FOUNDATION EDITION

VICTOR W. WATTON

Hodder & Stoughton
A MEMBER OF THE HODDER HEADLINE GROUP

ACKNOWLEDGEMENTS

The publishers would like to thank the following for permission to reproduce material in this book:

BUAV for the extract from a recent publication; Christian Education Movement for extracts from *What the Churches Say on Moral Issues*, reproduced by permission; T & T Clark for extracts from *The Third Reich and the Christian Churches* by P Matheson; Continuum Publishing for extracts from *The Catechism of the Catholic Church*; HarperCollins Publishers for extract from *Hope and Suffering* by Desmond Tutu; Muslim Educational Trust for extracts from *What Does Islam Say?* by Ibraham Hewitt; Oxford University Press for the extracts from *The Upanishads* translated by Patrick Olivelle (Oxford World's Classics, 1998) © Patrick Olivelle (1998), by permission of Oxford University Press; Pax Christi, USA for various extracts; Penguin UK for the extract from *Hinduism* by K M Sen (1961), reproduced by permission of Penguin Books; Polity Press for extract from *Sociology* by A Giddens; Transworld Publishers © Space Time Publications Ltd 1988. Extracted from *A Brief History of Time* by Stephen Hawking, published by Bantam Press, a division of Transworld Publishers. All rights reserved; SPCK for the extract from *Science and Creation* by J Polkinghorne; Quotations from the English translation of *The Catechism of the Catholic Church for Australia* © 1994 St Pauls, Strathfield, Australia/Libreria Editrice Vaticana, used with permission.

Scriptures quoted from The Holy Bible, New International Version by Hodder & Stoughton © 1973, 1978, 1984 International Bible Society, with permission; The Holy Qur'an, translated by Yusuf Ali © IPCI, with permission.

The publishers would like to thank the following individuals, institutions and companies for permission to reproduce photographs and illustrations in this book:

Achinto/Christian Aid/Still Pictures p42; AKG Photo London (Andre Normil) p120; Bridgeman Art Library pp16, 22, 65, 115; Circa Photo Library (Zbignieu Kosc) p12, (William Holtby) p14; Corbis pp44 (Joe McDonald), 45 (Frank Lane Picture Agency), 46 (John Periam, Cordaiy Photo Library Ltd), 47, 48 (Richard T Nowitz), 49 (David H Wells), 51 (Angelo Hornak), 54 (Humphrey Evans), 56, 60, 100, 103, 104, 109 (Reuters NewMedia Inc, 57 (David Rubinger), 67 (Ted Spiegel), 68 (Tiziana and Gianni Baldizzone), 70 (Flip Schulke), 76 (Bettman), 79 (David Reed), 83 (Eldad Rafaeli), 84, 85 (Hulton-Deutsche Collection), 97 (Stephanie Maze), 118 Gary Braasch, 119 (Kevin Schafer); Mark Edwards/Still Pictures pp36, 40; Eye Ubiquitous p10; Jewish National Fund p43; PA News p17, 18, 20, 21, 23, 27, 31, 52, 63, 71, 78, 81, 82, 86, 87, 88, 99, 106, 110, 111; David Rose p8; Peter Sanders p66; Science Photo Library (Martin Dohrn) p98, (Mehau Kulyk) 121, (David A Hardy) 123.

Every effort has been made to trace and acknowledge copyright. The publishers will be happy to include details of copyright holders it has not been possible to contact in subsequent editions.

Dedication
For my children and grandchildren – Simon, Rebecca, Timothy, Abigail, Peter, Benjamin and Kisa.

Orders: please contact Bookpoint Ltd, 130 Milton Park, Abingdon, Oxon OX14 4SB. Telephone: (44) 01235 827720, Fax: (44) 01235 400454. Lines are open from 9.00–6.00, Monday to Saturday, with a 24 hour message answering service. You can also order through our website www.hodderheadline.co.uk

British Library Cataloguing in Publication Data
A catalogue record for this title is available from The British Library

ISBN 0 340 850469

First published 2002
Impression number   10 9 8 7 6 5 4 3 2 1
Year   2006 2005 2004 2003 2002

Copyright © 2002 Victor W. Watton

All rights reserved. No part of this publication may be reproduced or transmitted in any form or by any means, electronic or mechanical, including photocopy, recording, or any information storage and retrieval system, without permission in writing from the publisher or under licence from the Copyright Licensing Agency Limited. Further details of such licences (for reprographic reproduction) may be obtained from the Copyright Licensing Agency Limited, of 90 Tottenham Court Road, London W1T 4LP.

Cover photo from Photodisk.
Printed in Italy for Hodder & Stoughton Educational, a division of Hodder Headline Plc, 338 Euston Road, London NW1 3BH.

CONTENTS

Preface		6
Introduction		7
Chapter 1 Religion and Social Responsibility		16
Factfile 1	How Christians make moral decisions	16
Factfile 2	The electoral system in the United Kingdom	20
Factfile 3	Christian belief in the separation of religion and politics	22
Factfile 4	Christian belief in involvement in politics	23
Factfile 5	The Welfare State	24
Factfile 6	The Christian basis of the Welfare State	26
Chapter 2 Religion and the Environment		29
Factfile 7	The dangers of pollution	29
Factfile 8	The problems of natural resources	32
Factfile 9	Non-religious arguments about the environment	33
Factfile 10	Christianity and the environment	35
Factfile 11	Islam and the environment	37
Factfile 12	Judaism and the environment	38
Factfile 13	Hinduism and the environment	40
Factfile 14	Religious groups and the environment	42
Factfile 15	Animal rights issues	44
Factfile 16	Christianity and animal rights	46
Factfile 17	Islam and animal rights	47
Factfile 18	Judaism and animal rights	48
Factfile 19	Hinduism and animal rights	49
Chapter 3 Religion: Peace and Conflict		51
Factfile 20	War and peace issues	51
Factfile 21	Christianity and war	54
Factfile 22	Islam and war	56
Factfile 23	Judaism and war	57
Factfile 24	Hinduism and war	58
Factfile 25	A religious group working for world peace	60
Factfile 26	Bullying	62
Factfile 27	Causes of conflict between families and friends	64
Factfile 28	Christianity and forgiveness	65
Factfile 29	Islam and forgiveness	66
Factfile 30	Judaism and forgiveness	67
Factfile 31	Hinduism and forgiveness	68

Chapter 4 Religion: Crime and Punishment   70

Factfile 32	Law and justice	70
Factfile 33	Christianity and justice	72
Factfile 34	Islam and justice	74
Factfile 35	Judaism and justice	76
Factfile 36	Hinduism and justice	78
Factfile 37	The nature of punishment	79
Factfile 38	Christianity and punishment	80
Factfile 39	Islam and punishment	82
Factfile 40	Judaism and punishment	83
Factfile 41	Hinduism and punishment	84
Factfile 42	Prisoners of conscience	85
Factfile 43	Capital punishment	87
Factfile 44	Christianity and capital punishment	88
Factfile 45	Islam and capital punishment	90
Factfile 46	Judaism and capital punishment	91
Factfile 47	Hinduism and capital punishment	92

Chapter 5 Religion and Medical Issues   94

Factfile 48	Medical treatments for infertility	94
Factfile 49	Christianity and infertility	96
Factfile 50	Islam and infertility	97
Factfile 51	Judaism and infertility	98
Factfile 52	Hinduism and infertility	99
Factfile 53	Genetic engineering	100
Factfile 54	Christianity and genetic engineering	102
Factfile 55	Islam and genetic engineering	104
Factfile 56	Judaism and genetic engineering	105
Factfile 57	Hinduism and genetic engineering	106
Factfile 58	Transplant surgery	107
Factfile 59	Christianity and transplant surgery	108
Factfile 60	Islam and transplant surgery	110
Factfile 61	Judaism and transplant surgery	111
Factfile 62	Hinduism and transplant surgery	112

Chapter 6 Religion and Science — 114

    Factfile 63   The biblical cosmology — 114
    Factfile 64   The Islamic cosmology — 116
    Factfile 65   The Jewish cosmology — 117
    Factfile 66   The Hindu cosmology — 118
    Factfile 67   The scientific cosmology — 119
    Factfile 68   Religious attitudes to the scientific cosmology — 120
    Factfile 69   How religion and science are connected — 123

Useful Addresses — 126

Index — 127

PREFACE

This book has been written for the new Edexcel GCSE Religious Studies Specification A. In conjunction with the *Teacher's Handbook*, also published by Hodder and Stoughton, it provides a complete resource for those preparing for the Edexcel Specification A Unit H, Religion and Society.

It provides resources on Christianity, Islam, Judaism and Hinduism which are colour coded by religion. Those wishing to study Buddhism or Sikhism alongside Christianity for Edexcel Specification A Unit H will find it helpful to use *Buddhism – A New Approach* or *Sikhism – A New Approach* in conjunction with this book. These are also published by Hodder and Stoughton.

There is no criticism of the religious attitudes covered in this book. This is to encourage students to think and evaluate for themselves. However, the *Teacher's Handbook* has photocopiable sheets of alternative viewpoints as well as revision files on every topic in Edexcel Unit H.

The word God is used throughout rather than using Allah in Islam and the Almighty in Judaism. This is to ensure that non-Muslim and non-Jewish students are not led into thinking that Jews or Muslims worship a different God.

When dates are given, the letters CE and BCE are used. These stand for Common Era and Before the Common Era, as AD and BC imply belief in Christianity.

I hope that students and teachers will find the book both useful and enjoyable and become more thinking and tolerant citizens as a result of their studies.

INTRODUCTION

It is important for you to know some basic facts about Christianity and one other religion before starting your GCSE.

CHRISTIANITY

Basic Christian beliefs

- Christians believe in one God.

- Christians believe God created everything.

- Christians believe God is loving and holy.

- Christians believe Jesus is God's son, and that he died on the cross and rose from the dead to give people life after death.

- Christians believe the Bible is the word of God.

How Christians make moral decisions

- All Christians believe decisions should be based on the Bible, especially the Ten Commandments and the teachings of Jesus;

- ROMAN CATHOLICS base moral decisions on the Pope's explanation of these teachings in the Catechism and letters called Encyclicals;

- ORTHODOX CHRISTIANS (and many Catholics) would ask their priest for advice;

- PROTESTANTS (Church of England, Methodists, Baptists, Pentecostals etc) make their decisions from the Bible but may be helped by advice from councils of Church leaders.

Factfiles concerning Christian beliefs and ideas are colour coded like this:

Examples:

Orthodox, Roman Catholic and some Evangelicals do not allow women priests, other Christians do.

Roman Catholics do not allow contraception, other Christians do.

Charismatics and many Evangelicals believe it is right to try to convert members of other religions, other Christians do not.

Catholic and Evangelical Christians believe homosexuality is condemned by God, other Christians do not.

Why there may be differences of opinion among Christians

Christians divided into Orthodox and Roman Catholic in 1054 because the Orthodox did not accept the leadership of the Pope.

Protestants divided from the Roman Catholics nearly 500 years ago because they thought all Christians were equal and therefore there should be no priests, or bishops, or popes.

Some Protestants are called Evangelicals because they believe all Christians should be 'born again' (conversion) and should accept everything the Bible says, so they disagree with other Protestants.

Some Christians are called charismatics. They believe that all Christians should have the gift of the Holy Spirit and be able to do things like speaking in tongues and healing people.

So Christians can disagree over:

- what they believe about the Church;
- what they believe about the Bible;
- what they believe about conversion;
- what they believe about the Holy Spirit.

Shared ministry is one way Churches are coming together.

ISLAM

Muslims call God, Allah. This is the Arabic word for God.

Basic Muslim beliefs

- The word Islam means giving yourself to God.

- Muslims believe that Islam is the first religion which God gave to Adam.

- Muslims believe there is only one God who created everything.

- Muslims believe Muhammad was God's last prophet who was given God's actual words in the Qur'an.

- Muslims believe that the way to heaven is to follow God's laws and the Five Pillars, all of which are based on the Qur'an.

Factfiles concerning Muslim beliefs and ideas are colour coded like this:

How Muslims make moral decisions

- Islam has laws about everything. These laws are called the SHARI'AH. They are based on the Qur'an and on what Muhammad said and did.

- To make moral decisions, Muslims follow the Shari'ah or ask a Muslim lawyer for advice.

- What Muslims are allowed to do is called HALAL.

- What Muslims are not allowed to do is called HARAM.

Examples:

Some Muslim Law Schools say eating shellfish is wrong, others say it is allowed.

Shi'ah Muslims allow men to have a temporary marriage, Sunnis do not.

Some Muslims say it is wrong to watch TV programmes showing the sexes mixing and women in non-Islamic clothes, others say it is all right as long as they are not doing evil things.

Why there may be differences of opinion among Muslims

- There are four schools of law in Islam which have slightly different forms of the Shari'ah.

- 85% of Muslims follow these law schools and are called Sunnis, but Shi'ah Muslims have their own different law school.

- The Shari'ah is over a thousand years old, so lawyers have to make their own decisions about things like watching television and they often disagree.

- Some Muslims think that all Muslims should be in one Muslim state, others think there should be separate states like Pakistan and Saudi Arabia.

The Holy Ka'aba, the centre of Islam.

10

JUDAISM

Jews believe that God's name is too holy for humans to use and so they often call God, the Almighty.

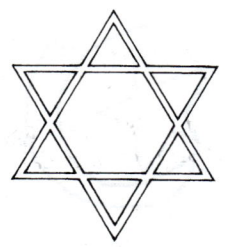

Basic Jewish beliefs

- Jews believe in one God.

- Jews believe God is holy and good.

- Jews believe God created the world and humans.

- Jews believe God made special agreements (covenants) with the Jewish people through Abraham and Moses.

- The covenant means that the Jews are the people of God if they follow the law God gave them in the Torah (the first five books of the Bible).

- The Jewish holy book is the same as the Christian Old Testament, but it is called the Tenakh.

Factfiles concerning Jewish beliefs and ideas are colour coded like this:

How Jews make moral decisions

- Jews base their moral decisions on the commands of God (MITZVOT) found in the Torah and explained in the TALMUD.

- If this does not help, they can ask rabbis who will use a guide book called HALAKHAH.

- Every Jewish community also has a law court called the BET DIN to help with problems.

Examples:

Some Jews (mainly Hasidic) believe Israel should not have been founded until the Messiah arrived.

Reform, Liberal and many Orthodox Jews believe Jews can wear whatever clothes they like, as long as men cover their heads, but the Hasidic and some Orthodox believe Jews must wear special clothes.

Reform and Liberal Jews give men and women equal divorce rights; Orthodox and Hasidic only allow divorce if the husband agrees.

Reform and Liberal Jews allow women to sit with men in the synagogues, Orthodox and Hasidic do not.

Why there may be differences of opinion among Jews

- For 2000 years, Jews had no country and Jews living in different areas had different interpretations of the Torah. These two groups are called the Sephardi and the Ashkenazi.

- About 300 years ago a group developed among the Ashkenazi which had slightly different ideas. They are called Hasidic Jews.

- About 150 years ago some Jews decided that the laws needed changing to fit in with modern life. These Jews are called Reform or Liberal Jews. Most Jews are Orthodox Jews who say that the laws cannot be changed.

Orthodox Jews praying at the Western Wall of the Temple of Jerusalem.

HINDUISM

Basic Hindu beliefs

- There are lots of Hindu religions, not just one.

- Some Hindus worship several gods, others worship only one.

- Most Hindus believe there is one spirit (Brahman) seen in the many gods and goddesses.

- Hindus have holy books such as the Vedas and the Gita, but they do not believe they are the word of God.

- Hindus believe life is like a wheel where you keep going round, being born, living, dying, being reborn (reincarnation). The aim of life for Hindus is to escape from the wheel (moksha).

- Many Hindus believe that what you do in one life decides what you will be reborn as in the next life. If you do your duty (dharma), you will keep being reborn into a better life until you can escape.

Factfiles concerning Hindu beliefs and ideas are colour coded like this:

How Hindus make moral decisions

- Dharma, based on Hindu laws in books like the Code of Manu, is taught to children by priests.

- For new situations, Hindus ask the advice of a holy person (swami or guru).

- Some Hindus base decisions on their own ideas of Hinduism.

Why there may be differences of opinion among Hindus

There are bound to be differences of opinion because there are so many forms of Hinduism such as Swaminarayan, Iskcon (Hare Krishna), Sai Baba.

Examples:

Some Hindus are vegetarian, others eat meat (but not beef).

Some Hindus refuse to drink alcohol, others believe it is a gift from God.

Some Hindus believe in the caste system, others (like the Swaminarayan) have rejected the caste system.

Some Hindus think every Hindu should get married, others think you can be a holy person instead.

A Hindu holy man at Varanasi.

Differences and similarities between religions

Although there are different religions, they often have the same ideas.

Because there are differences in a religion, people can sometimes agree with a person from another religion and disagree with a person from their own religion.

People have their own ideas and so they do not always believe all the things they are supposed to believe.

NON-RELIGIOUS PEOPLE AND MORAL ISSUES

It is possible to make moral decisions without religion. People who are not religious can make moral decisions by:

- looking at what the law says;

- looking at what will happen if they do something and deciding which decision will have the best results for the most people;

- looking at what seems to be the best decision and then working out what it would be like if everyone made that decision. For example, they would not steal because if everyone stole, no one would have anything.

LABOUR'S NEW SLEAZE
BOTH RELIGIOUS AND NON-RELIGIOUS PEOPLE ARGUE ABOUT THE MORALITY OF POLITICIANS

 RELIGION AND SOCIAL RESPONSIBILITY

FACTFILE 1

How Christians make moral decisions

BIBLE – THE HOLY BOOK OF CHRISTIANS WITH 66 BOOKS SPLIT INTO THE OLD TESTAMENT AND THE NEW TESTAMENT.

CHURCH – THE COMMUNITY OF CHRISTIANS (WITH A SMALL C, IT MEANS A CHRISTIAN PLACE OF WORSHIP).

CONSCIENCE – AN INNER FEELING OF THE RIGHTNESS OR WRONGNESS OF AN ACTION.

SITUATION ETHICS – THE IDEA THAT CHRISTIANS SHOULD BASE MORAL DECISIONS ON WHAT IS THE MOST LOVING THING TO DO IN A SITUATION.

ELECTORAL SYSTEM – THE WAY IN WHICH VOTING IS ORGANISED.

FIRST-PAST-THE-POST – THE VOTING SYSTEM WHERE WHOEVER GETS THE MOST VOTES IN A CONSTITUENCY (AREA REPRESENTED BY AN MP) WINS THE SEAT.

PROPORTIONAL REPRESENTATION – THE VOTING SYSTEM WHERE SEATS ARE DISTRIBUTED ACCORDING TO THE PROPORTION OF VOTES EACH PARTY GETS.

NATIONAL GOVERNMENT – THE GOVERNMENT HEADED BY THE PRIME MINISTER WHICH GOVERNS THE WHOLE COUNTRY.

LOCAL GOVERNMENT – THE LOCAL COUNCIL WHICH LOOKS AFTER LOCAL ISSUES SUCH AS EDUCATION AND REFUSE COLLECTION.

DECALOGUE – THE TEN COMMANDMENTS

GOLDEN RULE – THE TEACHING OF JESUS THAT PEOPLE SHOULD TREAT OTHERS AS THEY WOULD LIKE TO BE TREATED.

> The Methodist Church believes that the Bible is the main source for what Christians should believe and do.

From *What the Churches Say* second edition.

> The Bible is God's Word and so contains the truth about Christianity.

Catechism of the Catholic Church.

The Lindisfarne Gospels (698 CE) are the earliest copy of the Bible produced in England.

Christians base their moral decisions on three things:

1 The Authority of the Bible
The authority of the Bible means that the Bible is thought to be so important that what it says about how to behave must be believed – for example, if Christians want to know whether they should steal something, they would look at the Bible and decide not to steal because the Ten Commandments ban stealing.

The most important parts of the Bible for making moral decisions are the Ten Commandments (Decalogue) and the Sermon on the Mount given by Jesus.

There are some differences among Christians about how important the Bible is:

- some Christians believe the Bible is the word of God and is the only authority;
- some Christians believe that, although the Bible is the word of God, it needs to be explained by the Church;
- some Christians believe that the Bible needs to be explained in the light of modern society (for example, the Bible's teachings on women and slavery made sense when the Bible was written, but cannot be accepted today).

2 The Authority of the Church
Most Christians believe that the Church has the right to explain what the Bible means about how Christians should behave today.

> The Bible records God's contacts with people. It is not God's words.

David Jenkins, former Bishop of Durham, quoted in *Christians in Britain Today* D. Cush.

> The General Synod is the 'parliament' of the Church of England. It is a mixture of bishops, clergy (priests) and laity (ordinary church members). It meets twice a year and makes statements on what the Church thinks about moral issues.

From *What the Churches Say* second edition.

The General Synod makes recommendations on moral issues for members of the Church of England.

Some Churches give advice on moral issues through elected Assemblies (for example, The Church of England and the Methodist Church). The Roman Catholic Church gives teachings on moral issues through the Pope and the Council of Bishops.

Most Christians believe that God speaks to Christians today through the Church.

The Pope has the final responsibility for stating Roman Catholic views on moral issues.

3 The role of conscience

Everyone has a conscience which tells them whether something is right or wrong, and makes them feel guilty when they do something wrong. Many Christians believe that they should follow their conscience on moral issues.

> When the Pope and the bishops make decisions on beliefs or moral issues, they act as the Magisterium of the Church to give teachings which cannot be wrong.

Catechism of the Catholic Church.

An example of how Christians might use their conscience to make a moral decision would be:

- they think that God is telling them to kill doctors who perform abortions because such doctors are murderers;
- they read the Bible and look at Church teachings which tell them to obey the voice of God;
- their conscience, however, tells them that all murder is wrong and so God could not be telling them to murder, so they follow their conscience and do not murder the doctors.

When they make moral decisions:

- some Christians only use the Bible;
- some Christians only use the Church's teachings;
- some Christians only use their conscience;
- some Christians use the Bible or the Church, but only if their conscience agrees;
- some Christians use a mixture of Bible, Church and conscience.

> Pray for us. We are sure that we have a clear conscience and desire to live honourably in every way.

Hebrews 13:18

> Conscience is what allows people to decide whether their actions are right or wrong.

Sermon 1 – Bishop Butler (quoted in Dictionary of Christian Ethics).

> People should always follow their conscience as long as their conscience knows about the teachings of the Church.

Catechism of the Catholic Church.

> One of the teachers of the law came and heard them debating. Noticing that Jesus had given them a good answer, he asked him, 'Of all the commandments, which is the most important?'
>
> 'The most important one,' answered Jesus, 'is this: "Hear O Israel, the Lord our God, the Lord is one. Love the Lord your God with your heart and with all your soul and with all your mind and with all your strength." The second is this: "Love your neighbour as yourself." There is no commandment greater than these.'

Mark 12: 28–31

FACTFILE 2

THE ELECTORAL SYSTEM IN THE UNITED KINGDOM

The Cabinet is made up of the Prime Minister and the Ministers in charge of the main government departments and makes major government decisions.

The United Kingdom has two types of government:

National Government, known as the Government and led by the Prime Minister and the Cabinet, is responsible for the Civil Service, the Armed Forces and all the areas in the pie chart. It pays for these by taxes.

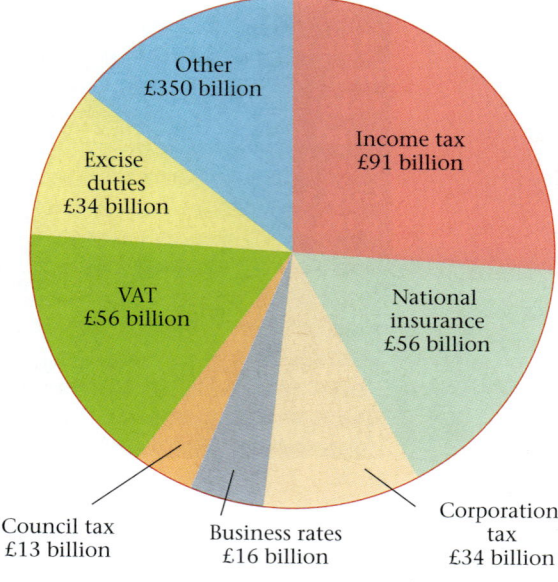

Tax income for the UK 1999–2000.

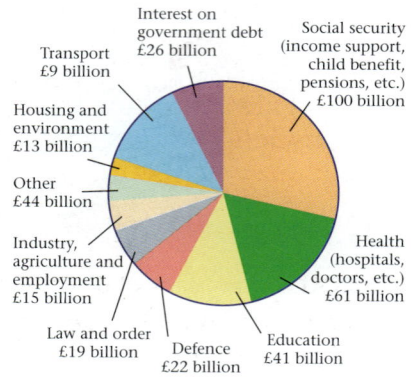

Tax expenditure for the UK 1999–2000.

20

Local Government, known as the Council, is led by the mayor. It is responsible for such things as refuse disposal and street cleaning which it pays for by the council tax. It looks after education, the police, and the fire service which are mainly paid for by National Government.

Scotland, Wales and Northern Ireland have their own regional assemblies led by a first minister and a cabinet.

There are also 74 MEPs who represent the United Kingdom in the European Parliament.

How MPs and Councillors are elected

MPs and councillors are elected by the **first-past-the-post system**. For MPs, the United Kingdom is divided up into 659 constituencies each with about 65,000 voters. Whichever candidate gains the most votes in a constituency becomes the MP even though more people voted against them than for them. In the 2001 election, Labour won 40.8% of the vote but gained 60.5% of the seats in the House of Commons. However, the constituency system means that people find it easy to contact their MP or councillor if they have a problem.

Ken Livingstone, the Mayor of London, was the first directly elected mayor in England.

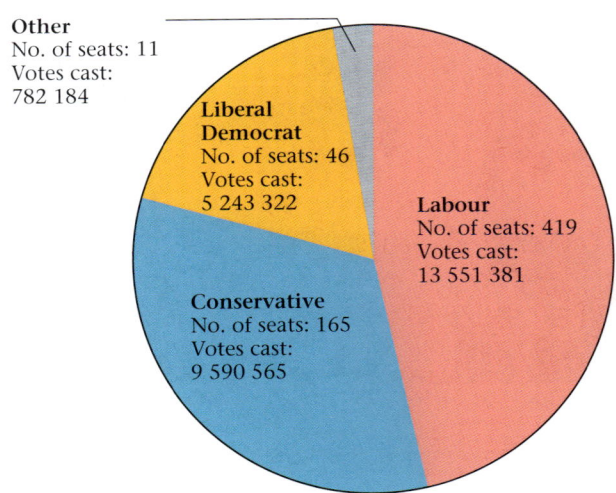

Votes and seats in the 1997 election.

MEPs and Scottish and Welsh assembly members are elected by **proportional representation** which means that the percentage of seats won is more closely connected to the percentage of the votes cast.

FACTFILE 3

CHRISTIAN BELIEF IN THE SEPARATION OF RELIGION AND POLITICS

Some Christians believe that Christianity should be kept separate from politics. They think that Christianity is about loving God and loving their neighbour while politics is about how society is run. They believe this because:

- Jesus said in Mark 12: 14-17 that Christians should give Caesar what is Caesar's and God what is God's which they think means religion and politics should be separate;
- St Paul said that Christians should obey the political leaders;
- Church leaders such as the Pope have always said that Christians should obey the leaders of the state;
- Religion and politics need to be kept separate to prevent fighting between different religions.

> 'Is it right to pay taxes to Caesar or not? Should we pay or shouldn't we?' But Jesus...asked, 'Bring me a denarius and let me look at it.' They brought the coin, and he asked them, 'Whose portrait is this? And whose inscription?'
>
> 'Caesar's,' they replied.
>
> Then Jesus said to them, 'Give to Caesar what is Caesar's and to God what is God's.'

Mark 12:14–17

> Everyone must submit himself to the governing authorities, for there is no authority except that which God has established. The authorities that exist have been established by God.

Romans 13:1

> Remind the people to be subject to rulers and authorities, to be obedient, to be ready to do whatever is good.

Titus 3:1

Jesus being asked about taxes.

> A Christian is a perfectly dutiful servant of all.

The Freedom of a Christian Man Martin Luther (1520).

> In their church activities, Catholics should not criticise the leaders of the state or their political views.

Statement by the Archbishop of Freiburg in June 1933 after the Nazis had come to power in Germany.

FACTFILE 4

CHRISTIAN BELIEF IN INVOLVEMENT IN POLITICS

Christians formed the Jubilee 2000 group to persuade the governments of rich countries to cancel the debts of poor countries.

Some Christians believe that Christianity is a whole way of life and that Christians should make their Christian beliefs a part of their politics. They believe this because:

- Jesus acted against the moneychangers in the Temple;
- Jesus said in the Sermon on the Mount that Christians cannot serve God and money, and serving politics is like serving money;
- St James said that Christian faith has to show itself in Christian actions, and the only way to put Christianity into action in the modern world is through politics;
- All the Churches say that Christians should work for world peace and a fairer sharing of wealth, which can only be done through politics.

> No one can serve two masters. Either he will hate the one and love the other, or he will be devoted to the one and despise the other. You cannot serve both God and money.

Matthew 6:24

> What good is it, my brothers, if a man claims to have faith but has no deeds? Can his faith save him? Suppose a brother or sister is without clothes and daily food. If one of you says to him, 'Go I wish you well; keep warm and well fed,' but does nothing about his physical needs, what good is it? In the same way, faith by itself, if not accompanied by action, is dead.

James 2:14–17

> We are Christians not only in church on Sunday ... We are Christians from Monday to Monday ... worshipping God and doing good work in our community.

Hope and Suffering, Desmond Tutu.

> The problem of rich and poor can only be solved by everyone working together. Poor people need to be united with each other, and rich people need to work with the poor to bring justice and peace.

Catechism of the Catholic Church.

FACTFILE 5

THE WELFARE STATE

The National Health Service provides free hospital treatment for everyone.

The Welfare State really began during the Second World War when the government produced the Beveridge Report into social conditions in Britain. It said there were five evil giants which had to be destroyed:

- **Want**   many people did not have enough to live on because they were unemployed, sick, widowed etc;

- **Disease**   many people could not afford to see a doctor when they were ill;

- **Ignorance**   most children left school without any secondary education;

- **Squalor**   many people were living in slums;

- **Idleness**   over 10% of the workers were unemployed.

The wartime coalition government of Conservatives and Labour attacked the giant of ignorance by making secondary education compulsory in 1944.

The Labour Government 1945–51 established the Welfare State by:

- removing want through providing pensions, sickness benefit, unemployment benefit;
- removing disease by setting up the National Health Service (NHS);
- removing squalor by demolishing slums and building council houses and new towns;
- removing idleness by setting up job creation schemes in areas of high unemployment.

The Welfare State today

The Welfare State provides:

- free education up to 18;
- free doctors and hospitals;
- social security so everyone has enough to live on;
- housing benefit and housing associations;
- job centres and help for setting up businesses.

> A welfare state is where governments provide help for the unemployed, the sick, the disabled and the elderly.

Sociology, A Giddens.

The Welfare State provides training so that everyone can find work.

FACTFILE 6

THE CHRISTIAN BASIS OF THE WELFARE STATE

Most of the people who set up the Welfare State were Christians. They wanted to set up the Welfare State because of Christian teachings such as the Ten Commandments:

Relations with God	Relations with other people
Worship one God only	Honour your parents
Do not worship idols	Do not murder
Do not swear using God's name	Do not steal
Keep the Sabbath day holy	Do not commit adultery
	Do not give false evidence
	Do not covet other people's belongings

How could Christians honour old people without giving them pensions? Refusing to help the poor is like stealing from them.

In the same way **the Golden Rule** of Jesus that Christians should treat other people as they would like to be treated is best carried out by the Welfare State.

The Golden Rule

So in everything, do to others what you would have them do to you, for this sums up the Law and the prophets.

Matthew 7:12

Many state schools were founded by Christian Churches who are often still involved in the way they are run.

26

Jesus said that Christians should feed the hungry, clothe the naked and help the sick in the Parable of the Sheep and the Goats and this is best done by the Welfare State.

Christians were already working for the Welfare State through Church schools, orphanages, hospitals etc.

Donald Soper was a leading Methodist minister.

The Parable of the Sheep and the Goats

When the Son of Man comes in his glory, and all the angels with him, he will sit on his throne in heavenly glory. All the nations will be gathered before him, and he will separate the people one from another as a shepherd separates the sheep from the goats. He will put the sheep on his right and the goats on his left.

Then the King will say to those on his right, 'Come, you who are blessed by my Father; take your inheritance, the kingdom prepared for you since the creation of the world. For I was hungry and you gave me something to eat, I was thirsty and you gave me something to drink, I was a stranger and you invited me in, I needed clothes and you clothed me, I was sick and you looked after me, I was in prison and you came to visit me.'

Then the righteous will answer him, 'Lord, when did we see you hungry and feed you, or thirsty and give you something to drink? When did we see you a stranger and invite you in, or needing clothes and clothe you? When did we see you sick or in prison and visit you?'

The King will reply, 'I tell you the truth, whatever you did for the least of these brothers of mine, you did for me.'

Then he will say to those on his left, 'Depart from me, you who are cursed, into the eternal fire prepared for the devil and his angels. For I was hungry and you gave me nothing to eat, I was thirsty and you gave me nothing to drink, I was a stranger and you did not invite me in, I needed clothes and you did not clothe me, I was sick and in prison and you did not look after me.'

They also will answer, 'Lord, when did I see you hungry or thirsty or a stranger or needing clothes or sick or in prison, and did not help you?'

He will reply, 'I tell you the truth, whatever you did not do for one of the least of these, you did not do for me.'

Matthew 25:37–40

'I thank God for the Welfare State,' declared Donald Soper.

Quoted in *A History of English Christianity*, A Hastings.

People cannot make money without thinking of the needs of others. An efficient society needs good public services.

Catechism of the Catholic Church.

27

QUESTIONS

Factfile 1 How Christians make moral decisions

1 Give an outline of one way in which a Christian would make a moral decision.

2 Give two reasons why Christians would use the Bible when making moral decisions.

3 Give two reasons for thinking that conscience is the best way to decide what is right and what is wrong.

4 Give two reasons for thinking that conscience is not the best way to decide what is right and what is wrong.

Factfile 2 The electoral system in the United Kingdom

1 For what things is national government responsible?

2 For what things is local government responsible?

3 Have a class discussion on why it is important to vote in elections.

Factfiles 3 Christian belief in the separation of religion and politics and 4 Christian belief in involvement in politics

1 Give three reasons why some Christians think Christianity should be kept out of politics.

2 Give three reasons why some Christians think Christianity should be involved in politics.

Factfile 5 The Welfare State

1 Name four things provided by the Welfare State.

2 Give three reasons why the United Kingdom began a Welfare State.

3 Have a class discussion on whether it is important to have a Welfare State.

Factfile 6 The Christian basis of the Welfare State

1 Write out the main points of the Parable of the Sheep and the Goats.

2 'Christians should not use private hospitals.'

   a) Give two reasons for agreeing with this statement.

   b) Give two reasons for disagreeing with this statement.

RELIGION AND THE ENVIRONMENT

POLLUTION – THE CONTAMINATION/DEGRADATION OF THE ENVIRONMENT.

GREENHOUSE EFFECT – THE TRAPPING OF CARBON DIOXIDE IN THE ATMOSPHERE, WHICH IS THOUGHT TO INCREASE THE EARTH'S TEMPERATURE.

ACID RAIN – POLLUTANTS SUCH AS COAL SMOKE RELEASE SULPHURIC AND NITRIC ACID, WHICH MAKE RAIN MORE ACIDIC.

NATURAL RESOURCES – NATURALLY OCCURRING MATERIALS, SUCH AS OIL AND FERTILE LAND, WHICH CAN BE USED BY HUMANS.

CREATION – THE ACT OF CREATING THE UNIVERSE, OR THE UNIVERSE WHICH HAS BEEN CREATED.

STEWARDSHIP – LOOKING AFTER SOMETHING SO THAT IT CAN BE PASSED ON TO THE NEXT GENERATION.

ENVIRONMENT – THE SURROUNDINGS IN WHICH PLANTS AND ANIMALS LIVE AND WHICH THEY DEPEND ON TO CONTINUE LIVING.

CONSERVATION – PROTECTING AND PRESERVING NATURAL RESOURCES AND THE ENVIRONMENT.

ANIMAL RIGHTS – THE BELIEF THAT ANIMALS HAVE RIGHTS WHICH SHOULD NOT BE EXPLOITED BY HUMANS.

The earth is an ecosystem where everything depends on everything else, for example animals produce nitrogen in excretion which feeds plants, animals eat the plants and produce nitrogen, etc. Changes to an ecosystem can cause major problems.

The main problems caused by pollution are:

- **The Greenhouse Effect**
Burning fuels like gas, oil and coal makes carbon dioxide which acts like the glass of a greenhouse letting the sun's heat in, but stopping it from getting out.

FACTFILE 7

THE DANGERS OF POLLUTION

This is making the earth heat up (global warming). Some scientists think the average temperature in England will rise by two degrees Celsius in the next fifty years. They think this will melt the ice at the north and south poles and cause massive flooding.

- **Acid Rain**

As well as producing carbon dioxide, burning oil, gas, and coal puts more acid into the atmosphere so that the rainfall becomes acidic and can burn things. Forests in Sweden are being destroyed by Britain's use of fuel.

- **Eutrophication**

Using fertilisers on farms and sewage disposal are putting too much nitrogen into streams and rivers making plants grow so fast that fish cannot get enough oxygen. The nitrogen also pollutes water supplies.

Nuclear power stations, such as this one at Hartlepool, could help to reduce the greenhouse effect.

Some people think the floods of autumn 2000 were a sign of the likely effects of global warming.

- **Deforestation**
Trees are being cut down and not replaced. This leads to soil disappearing so that land becomes like a desert (desertification). It also leads to an increase of nitrogen and a decrease of oxygen in the atmosphere.

- **Radioactive pollution**
Nuclear power stations have been built because they do not produce carbon dioxide or acid rain, but they do produce nuclear waste which will take hundreds of thousands of years to become safe for humans.

Professor Brian Lee, an expert with the Environment Agency, claims that global warming will lead to serious flooding in Britain every year. He thinks that Britain should have a national disaster agency to deal with the effects of global warming.

The Times, 14 December 2000.

FACTFILE 8

THE PROBLEMS OF NATURAL RESOURCES

Natural resources can be divided into two types:

Renewable resources are resources which can replace themselves after they have been used. They will not die out and using them causes no problems. Examples of renewable resources are: wind power, solar power, water power and such products as sugar cane being used instead of petrol.

These pipelines are taking oil from the North Sea which can never be replaced.

Finite or non-renewable resources are resources which are gone forever once they are used. Such things as oil, gas, coal, iron and tin are finite resources. Finite resources are used for not only cars and heating, but also for everything made of metal or plastic. If we keep using these resources, they will disappear and there will be nothing to make cars, televisions, washing machines etc.

> The Government of Cambodia has made the British-based environmental charity, Global Witness, its inspector of illegal logging. It will help the Government to stop the illegal cutting down of hardwood trees (which take hundreds of years to grow).

The Times, 3 December 1999.

FACTFILE 9

NON-RELIGIOUS ARGUMENTS ABOUT THE ENVIRONMENT

There are many arguments about what should be done to save the environment:

1. Many people think that the governments of the world need to act. In 1997, the Kyoto Agreement was signed by 55 individual countries who agreed to cut the amount of greenhouse gases they produce by 5.2% per year. However, the world's biggest greenhouse gas polluter, the USA, would not sign; instead they are increasing the size of their forests to produce the same effect (trees can turn carbon dioxide into oxygen).

> The Environment Minister said yesterday that Britain will soon have reduced its greenhouse gases by 23% and called on other countries to do the same.

The Times, 18 November 2000.

Britain's first power station producing electricity from waste is an attempt to preserve resources.

2. Some scientists think that the use of science and technology will change from using finite to renewable resources, and the use of re-cycling, will solve the problems;
   - Electricity can now be produced by wind, sun, water, waves and tides.
   - Cars can be powered by water, sugar cane or electric batteries.
   - Some cars are now made of 75% recycled materials.

- The pollution produced by 50 cars made in 1999 is only the same as that produced by one car made in 1976.
- By 2010, the pollution from cars will be 75% less than it was in 1992.

3 Some people think that the only way to solve the problem of pollution is for people to change their life-styles – for example ride bikes instead of using cars, use cotton and wool instead of polyester and viscose etc.

There are now many wind farms, like this one in Cornwall, producing pollution-free, renewable electricity.

Christians believe that they have to care for the environment because:

- the Bible says that God created the world as a good place;
- God made humans as stewards of the earth which means that they have to look after it;
- Christians say that Jesus told the Parable of the Talents to tell Christians that they have to leave the earth in a better condition than they found it.

> God made the universe and all its parts work together. Men and women should be stewards of the earth's resources, not exploiters.

Christian Faith Concerning the Environment – Methodist Conference 1991.

FACTFILE 10

CHRISTIANITY AND THE ENVIRONMENT

> God blessed them and said to them, 'Be fruitful and increase in number. Rule over the fish of the sea and the birds of the air and over every living creature that moves on the ground.'

Genesis 1:28

> When I consider your heavens, the work of your fingers ... what is man that you are mindful of him? You made him a little lower than the heavenly beings ... You made him rule over the work of your hands; you put everything under his feet.

Psalm 8:3–6

Would Christian teachings make industry more environmentally friendly?

35

To leave the earth a better place than they found it, Christians must:

- work to reduce pollution and the use of finite resources;
- work for a fairer sharing of the earth's resources;
- support groups working to improve the environment.

However, Christians believe that people are more important than things because people have been put in charge of the earth by God. So, for example, Christians would not shut down a factory employing 300 people just to reduce pollution.

> This Synod urges Her Majesty's Government to take all possible steps to reduce pollution and to bring about a fair use of the earth's energy resources.

Motion at the General Synod of the Church of England 1992.

> Although God has put humans in charge of the resources of the universe, this power must be used with concern for the rights of neighbours and future generations.

Catechism of the Catholic Church.

Solar-powered houses help to preserve resources.

FACTFILE 11

ISLAM AND THE ENVIRONMENT

Islam teaches that Muslims have been placed in charge of the earth and its resources by God, and that they have a duty to look after the earth in the way God wishes. This means trying to reduce pollution and the use of finite resources.

Muslims believe this because:

- the one God made one universe and there is a unity in creation (Tawhid);
- Tawhid means that the whole universe is in balance like an ecosystem;
- the Qur'an says that God made humans as his Khalifah to look after the earth;
- Islam teaches that this life is a test, and at the Day of Judgement, Muslims will be judged on how they have looked after the earth.

However, human needs must always come first for Muslims.

> **Behold thy Lord said to the angels, 'I will create a vice-gerent on earth.' … And He taught Adam the nature of all things … And behold, He said to the angels: 'Bow down to Adam.' And they bowed down: Not so Iblis: he refused and was haughty: He was of those who reject the faith.**
>
> Surah 2:30–34

> **The sun and the moon follow courses exactly computed; And the herbs and the trees – both alike bow in adoration. And the firmament has He raised high, and He has set up the balance in order that ye may not transgress balance.**
>
> Surah 55:5–8

> **Behold in the creation of the heavens and the earth; in the alternation of the night and the day … in the rain which God sends down from the skies, and the life which He gives therewith … in the beasts of all kinds that He scatters through the earth; in the change of the wind and the clouds … here indeed are signs for a people that are wise.**
>
> Surah 2:164

> The earth has been created by Allah and humans have been made God's agents to look after and protect the natural balance of the environment.
>
> *What does Islam Say?* Ibrahim Hewitt.

FACTFILE 12

JUDAISM AND THE ENVIRONMENT

Judaism teaches that God created the earth and gave humans the task of being stewards of the earth to look after it well. They believe this because:

- Genesis chapters 1 and 2 say that God created the earth and gave Adam control of plants and animals;
- there is a law in the Torah that every town must be surrounded by an area of parkland;

The Tees Barrage is helping to reduce pollution and prevent floods.

> God blessed them (male and female) and said to them, 'Be fruitful and increase in number; fill the earth and subdue it. Rule over the fish ... and the birds ... and over every living creature.'

Genesis 1:28

- the Torah and Talmud say that nothing that is useful should be destroyed except to provide for human need;
- the New Year for trees encourages respect for the environment as Jews have to plant trees where they are needed;
- the Torah orders a Jubilee Year every fifty years when the land must be rested to re-charge its batteries.

> When you lay siege to a city for a long time ... do not destroy its trees by putting an axe to them ... Do not cut them down. Are the trees of the fields people, that you should besiege them?

Deuteronomy 20:19

> Command the Israelites to give the Levites towns ... And give them pasture-lands around the towns ... The pasture-lands around the towns will extend fifteen hundred feet from the town wall.

Numbers 35:2

Jews must therefore support the work of conservation groups, but they must always put human interests first.

> People are not just part of the ecosystem. As far as Jews are concerned, humans have the highest value and their interests must come first in environmental concerns.

Moral Issues in Judaism, Arye Forta.

> The earth is the Lord's, and everything in it, the world and all who live in it.

Psalm 24:1

FACTFILE 13

HINDUISM AND THE ENVIRONMENT

Hinduism teaches that there is a oneness in the universe created by God. Humans must not exploit nature, but must work with nature and respect plants and animals. Hindus believe this because:

- there is an eternal law of nature and so joining with nature helps people to find peace;
- God is present in the universe he has created, so it must be respected;
- the teachings on ahimsa (non-violence) and the fact that the gods often appeared as animals means that animals, especially cows, must be respected;

> The waters are the body of breath, and the moon up there is its luminous appearance. So, the extent of the waters and of that moon is the same as the extent of breath. Now, all of these are of equal extent, all are without limit. So those who venerate them as finite win only a limited world, whereas those who venerate them as infinite win a world without limit.

Upanishad 1:5:13

> Peace of sky, peace of mid-region,
>
> peace of earth, peace of waters, peace of plants.
>
> Peace of trees, peace of all gods, peace of Brahman,
>
> peace of the universe, peace of peace,
>
> May that peace come to me.

Yajur-veda VS 36.17

The Hindu custom of planting trees helps to make the soil more fertile.

- the third ashrama teaches that living in the forest can help people to find God;
- many Hindu holy men, including the Buddha, have found God whilst sitting under trees;
- a Hindu holy man had a vision in the fifteenth century that human beings would be destroyed because they had destroyed nature.

Hindus must respect the environment, but there is disagreement between those who think humans are the most advanced form of life and so can use the environment as they wish and those who think that all forms of life have equal rights.

> May men and oxen both plough in contentment, in contentment the plough cleave the furrow. Auspicious furrow, we venerate you. We pray you, bless us and bring us abundant harvests.

Rig Veda IV.57

> What makes Indian society different is that it finds its inspiration in the forest, not the city. The peace of the forest has helped the human mind to develop.

Rabindranath Tagore in *Tapovana*.

FACTFILE 14

RELIGIOUS GROUPS AND THE ENVIRONMENT

A Christian Aid project of planting seedlings and fruit bushes to prevent soil erosion.

All religions have groups helping to conserve the environment:

- Christian Aid makes sure that its development work protects the environment;
- Target Earth is a Christian group which buys up land to re-forest and protect endangered species;
- Muslim Aid makes sure that its development work in places like Afghanistan conserves the environment;
- Judaism has groups like the Hadassah;
- the Chipko Movement is a Hindu tree-hugging group founded to prevent trees being cut down.

Target Earth provides opportunities for Christians who care about God's earth. We are enthusiastic that this group will lead Christians forward into the new millenium.

Tom Sine and Christine Aroney-Sine, Global development specialists.

In 1993, the Eden Conservancy was established to deal with the problems of de-forestation by buying up endangered land to protect God's good creation. One such property is 8,000 acres of rainforest in Belize, South America which, when protected, will remind people of the majesty and beauty of God's handiwork.

From a Target Earth pamphlet.

The work of the Jewish National Fund (JNF)

Jews from all over the world regard Israel as a holy land and want to remove pollution and conserve resources. They do this by giving to the Jewish National Fund (JNF), a religious organisation which works according to the mitzvot of Judaism.

The JNF:

- has planted 200 million trees in Israel to reduce the greenhouse effect and to reclaim land from the desert;
- has developed a process called 'savannisation' which uses available water to make the desert useful for farming;
- has built reservoirs and dams to use the storm water which usually disappears into the desert;
- is working to make dangerous places such as landfill sites, waste dumps and old quarries safe and attractive.

Rolling back the desert in the northern sections of the Negev.

FACTFILE 15

Animal rights issues

Animal rights means the idea that animals have rights that humans should not destroy.

Can animals have rights?

Some people think animals cannot have rights because:

- only those who can protect their rights can have rights and animals cannot protect their rights;
- having rights involves there being a choice about how to behave and animals, unlike humans, cannot choose how they live.

Some people think animals can have rights because:

- very young children still have rights even though they cannot protect them;
- very young children cannot choose how they live.

Most people think that humans have a moral duty not to abuse animals whether or not they believe animals have rights.

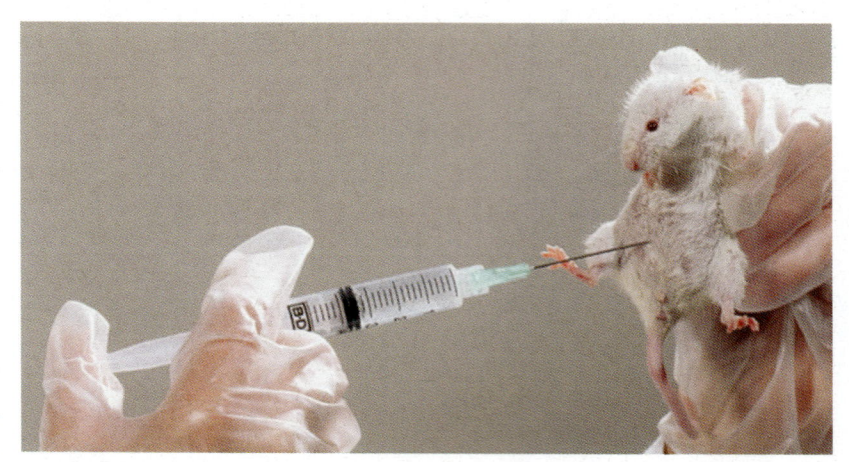

A scientist searching for a cure for Aids injects a mouse.

Should animals be used in experiments?

For experimenting on animals	Against experimenting on animals
• Animals do not have rights	• Animals should not be abused
• Human health comes first	• Animal researchers become sub-human
• Experiments on animals have led to cures for diseases	• Preventing people from getting diseases would be better
• Research on animals stops drugs from harming humans	• Drugs should not be used if they need animal research.

Should animals be used for food?

Arguments for eating animals	Arguments against eating animals
• Humans have meat-eating teeth	• Humans can live without meat
• Other animals eat meat	• Some animals do not eat meat
• Killing animals for food is done without pain	• Killing animals always causes suffering
• There would be a lot of cruelty if farmers left millions of animals to starve.	• Humans could find a way to deal with the problem of having too many animals.

More and more people believe we should only eat eggs from hens that live a normal life (free range).

There are: 44 million sheep 12 million cattle 8 million pigs 128 million hens, ducks, geese kept on farms in Britain

Source: Meat and Livestock Commission.

Antibiotics and successful treatments for asthma, diabetes and leukaemia came from research on animals.

Source: The Biomedical Research Trust.

Vivisection means cutting up living animals in experiments. Between 100 and 200 million painful experiments take place every year with over 2.5 million happening in Britain.

Source: British Union for the Abolition of Vivisection (BUAV).

FACTFILE 16

CHRISTIANITY AND ANIMAL RIGHTS

> Then God said, 'Let us make man in our image, in our likeness, and let them rule over the fish of the sea and the birds of the air, over the livestock, over all the earth, and over all the creatures that move along the ground.'

Genesis 1:26

> Are not two sparrows sold for a penny? Yet not one of them will fall to the ground apart from the will of your father.

Matthew 10:29

> Although Christianity has always regarded animals as an important part of God's creation, they do not have the same rights as humans because humans have been made in God's image.

Our Responsibility for the Living Environment report by the Church of England Board for Social Responsibility.

> Christians should be kind to all God's creatures.

General Advice to Quakers 1928

Most Christians believe that humans should not be cruel to animals. They believe that:

- farmers should look after animals humanely;
- animals for food should be killed without pain;
- scientists should only use animals for medical experiments when there is no other method.

However, they believe that humans can use animals for food and medical experiments because:

- God put humans in control of animals;
- only humans have rights because they are the only ones made in the image of God;
- humans are God's stewards of the earth and so must care for animals.

Some Christians are against animals being used for food or experiments because:

- God created animals;
- humans are God's stewards and so must care for animals;
- Christians should never be cruel and it is impossible to use animals for food or experiments without being cruel to them.

There is a Christian tradition of preventing cruelty to animals.

Muslims believe that humans should not be cruel to animals. They believe that:

- farmers should look after animals humanely;
- animals for food should be killed without pain;
- scientists should only use animals for medical experiments when there is no other method.

However, they believe humans can use animals for food and medical experiments because:

- the Qur'an teaches that animals have feelings and must be killed painlessly;
- the Qur'an says that Muslims can use certain animals for food;
- the Shari'ah says that animals can be used for medical experiments.

FACTFILE 17

ISLAM AND ANIMAL RIGHTS

> There is not an animal that lives on the earth, nor a being that flies on its wings, but forms part of communities like you. Nothing have we omitted from the Book and they all shall be gathered to their Lord in the end.

Surah 6:38

> Seest thou not that it is God whose praises all beings in the heavens and on earth do celebrate, and the birds of the air with wings outspread? Each one knows its own mode of prayer and praise. And God knows well all that they do.

Surah 24:41

> Allah's stewards have a duty to preserve the unity of his creation by protecting and conserving plants and animals.

Muslim Declaration from Assisi 1986

> It is wrong to slaughter animals where other animals can see it. It is wrong for a person to slaughter an animal they have brought up.

Articles of Islamic Acts, the Al-Khoei Foundation.

47

FACTFILE 18

JUDAISM AND ANIMAL RIGHTS

Most Jews believe that humans should not be cruel to animals. They believe that:

- farmers should look after animals humanely;
- animals for food should be killed without pain;
- scientists should only use animals for medical experiments when there is no other method.

However, they believe that humans can use animals for food and medical experiments because:

- God put humans in control of animals;
- only humans have rights because they are the only ones made in the image of God;
- the Torah bans cruelty to animals;
- the Talmud has laws to make farmers treat their animals well.

Some Jews are vegetarians because they think it is impossible to eat meat without being involved in cruelty to animals.

> Then God said, 'Let us make man in our image, in our likeness, and let them rule over the fish of the sea and the birds of the air, over the livestock, over all the earth, and over all the creatures that move along the ground.'

Genesis 1:26

> A righteous man cares for the needs of his animal.

Proverbs 12:10

> The fear and dread of you will fall upon all the beasts of the earth and all the birds of the air, upon every creature that moves along the ground, and upon all the fish of the sea, they are given into your hands. Everything that lives and moves will be food for you.

Genesis 9:2–3

> Children should be taught to respect animals. Children who enjoy making beetles suffer will not care about human suffering when they grow up.

Statement by Rabbi Samson Raphael Hirsch.

Kosher shops ensure that food has been prepared properly and humanely.

FACTFILE 19

HINDUISM AND ANIMAL RIGHTS

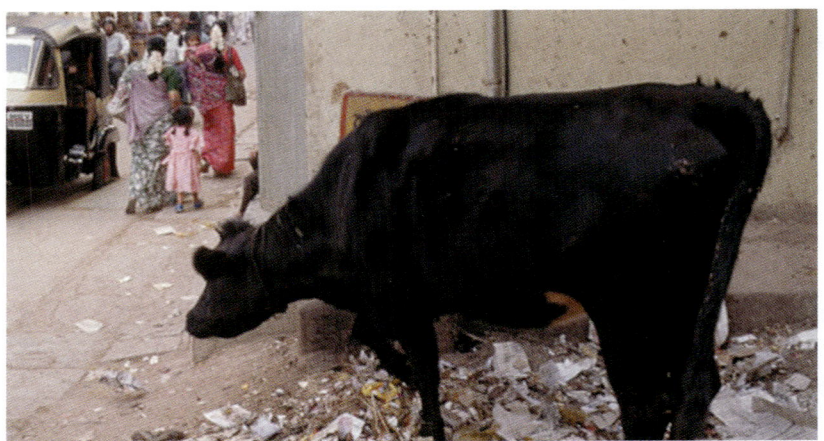

Cows are allowed to roam freely in India.

Hindus will not kill cows and so no Hindus eat beef. Cows are protected animals in India. Hindus believe cows are sacred because:

- the God Shiva rides on a bull;
- the God Krishna was a cowherd when he came to earth;
- cows provide dairy foods (milk, cheese etc), transport and fuel (dried dung).

Hindus believe animals have rights and should be protected from cruelty. They believe this because:

- they believe God is in all creatures;
- ahimsa means that violence against animals is wrong;
- the belief in rebirth means that killing an animal could be killing a relative;
- animals are closely related to the gods, for example, Ganesha the elephant god and Hanuman the monkey god.

> A householder should regard deer, camels, donkeys, mice, snakes, birds and bees as his sons: for what difference is there between his sons and them?

Bhagavata Purana 7, 14, 9

> Sweet be our Father heaven to us.
>
> For us may the forest tree be full of sweetness,
>
> full of sweetness the sun,
>
> and full of sweetness the cows for us.

Rig Veda I.90:6–8

> He who offers to me with devotion only a leaf, or a flower, or a fruit, or even a little water, this I accept from that yearning soul because with a pure heart it was offered with love. Whatever you do, or eat, or give, or offer in adoration, let it be an offering to me.

Bhagavad Gita 9:26–27

> In the country of Couche in India, they will kill nothing and have hospitals for sheep, goats, dogs, cats and all other living creatures.

From the records of the travels of Ralph Fetch who visited India in the sixteenth century (quoted from *Hinduism*, K M Sen).

> He serves God best who is kind to all living creatures.

Swami Vivekananda (quoted from *Themes and Issues in Hinduism*, P Bowen).

Questions

Factfiles 7 The dangers of pollution, 8 The problems of natural resources and 9 Non-religious arguments about the environment

1. What is an ecosystem?
2. Make a list of things people are doing which will damage the earth's ecosystem.
3. Give three reasons why resources could be a problem in the future.
4. Make a list of things people are doing to reduce pollution.
5. Make a list of things people are doing to reduce the problem of resources.

Factfile 10 Christianity and the environment

1. What is meant by Christian stewardship?
2. State two biblical teachings on stewardship.
3. State three things you should do to improve the environment.

Factfiles 11, 12, 13 Islam, Judaism and Hinduism and the environment

1. Choose one religion other than Christianity and write down what it teaches about the correct use of the environment.
2. 'If religious people took their religion seriously, there would be no environmental problems.'
   a) Give two reasons for agreeing with this statement.
   b) Give two reasons for disagreeing with this statement.

Factfile 14 Religious groups and the environment

List four things a religious group is doing to improve the environment.

Factfile 15 Animal rights issues

1. Give three arguments in favour of research on animals.
2. Give three arguments against research on animals.

Factfile 16 Christianity and animal rights

1. Outline Christian teachings on animal rights.
2. Give two reasons why some Christians are against research on animals.

Factfile 17, 18, 19 Islam, Judaism and Hinduism and animal rights

1. Choose one religion other than Christianity and outline its teachings on animal rights.
2. 'Religion does not help animal rights.'
   a) Give two reasons for agreeing with this statement.
   b) Give two reasons for disagreeing with this statement.

3 RELIGION: PEACE AND CONFLICT

NUCLEAR WEAPONS – WEAPONS BASED ON ATOMIC FISSION OR FUSION.

OTHER WEAPONS OF MASS DESTRUCTION – NON-NUCLEAR WEAPONS WHICH CAN DESTROY LARGE AREAS AND/OR LARGE NUMBERS OF PEOPLE E.G. CHEMICAL WEAPONS.

PACIFISM – REFUSING TO FIGHT IN WARS.

JUST WAR – A WAR THAT IS FOUGHT FOR THE RIGHT REASONS AND IN A RIGHT WAY.

WORLD PEACE – THE BASIC AIM OF THE UNITED NATIONS TO REMOVE THE CAUSES OF WAR.

BULLYING – INTIMIDATING/FRIGHTENING PEOPLE WEAKER THAN YOURSELF.

FORGIVENESS – THE ACT OF STOPPING BLAMING SOMEONE AND/OR PARDONING THEM FOR WHAT THEY HAVE DONE WRONG.

RECONCILIATION – BRINGING TOGETHER PEOPLE WHO WERE OPPOSED TO EACH OTHER.

In 1945, the United Nations was set up to keep world peace and stop wars.

FACTFILE 20

WAR AND PEACE ISSUES

The United Nations Headquarters in New York is on independent territory given to the UN by the United States government.

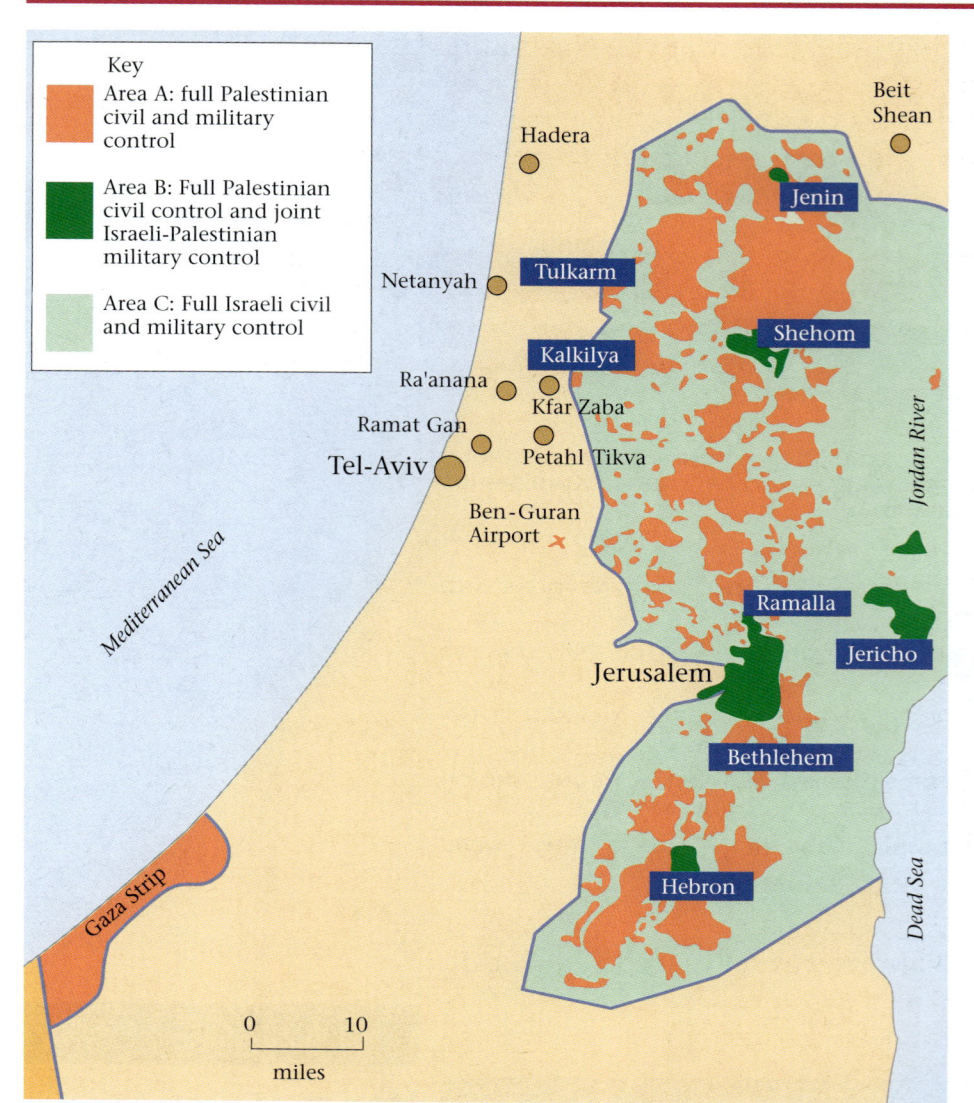

Key
- Area A: full Palestinian civil and military control
- Area B: Full Palestinian civil control and joint Israeli-Palestinian military control
- Area C: Full Israeli civil and military control

However, since 1945, there have been many wars. Two major ones were the Korean War (1950–53) and the Vietnam War (1961–75). There are still many areas of conflict in the world today. You have to know the name of one and the reasons for another.

1 Israel and Palestine

There is conflict between Israel and the Palestinian people in the Middle East. The Palestinians want their own Palestinian state in areas which are controlled by Israel. This was partly agreed in the Oslo Agreement (1993–5) but it has still not been put into practice.

The Holy Mount in Jerusalem causes trouble because it is claimed by Jews, Christians and Muslims.

The main reasons for the conflict are:

- The Jews and the Arabs both regard the same area as their homeland.
- Israel ruled the area from 1000 BCE to 132 CE and the Palestinians from 635 CE to the First World War.
- Britain captured Palestine during the First World War and promised a homeland for both the Israelis and the Palestinians.

- Many Jews came to the area to escape the Nazis and after they revolted against the British, they established the State of Israel in 1947 which was recognised by the United nations, but not by the Palestinians.
- Israel occupied the rest of Palestine after a war in 1967.
- The Palestinians want their land back, but Israel will only give it back if the Palestinians accept the existence of Israel.

2 Kashmir

Kashmir has been fought over since the British left India in 1947. Both India and Pakistan claim the area and a full-scale war could break out between these countries at any time.

The main reasons for this conflict are:

- When Britain left India in 1947, the majority Muslim areas of the North did not join India but became the Muslim state of West Pakistan and East Pakistan (now Bangladesh).
- Kashmir was majority Muslim, but did not join Pakistan because the ruler was Hindu and there were a lot of Hindus in Kashmir.
- Ever since Pakistani and Muslim Kashmiri rebels have been fighting to make Kashmir an independent Muslim state.

A major problem for world peace is that so many countries have weapons of mass destruction (such as nuclear and chemical weapons) which could destroy the world.

Israel, India and Pakistan all have nuclear weapons.

> The American Secretary of State, Colin Powell, told reporters that the United States needs a missile defence system to protect itself from attack by Third World nuclear states.

Adapted from a *Times* report, 18 December 2000.

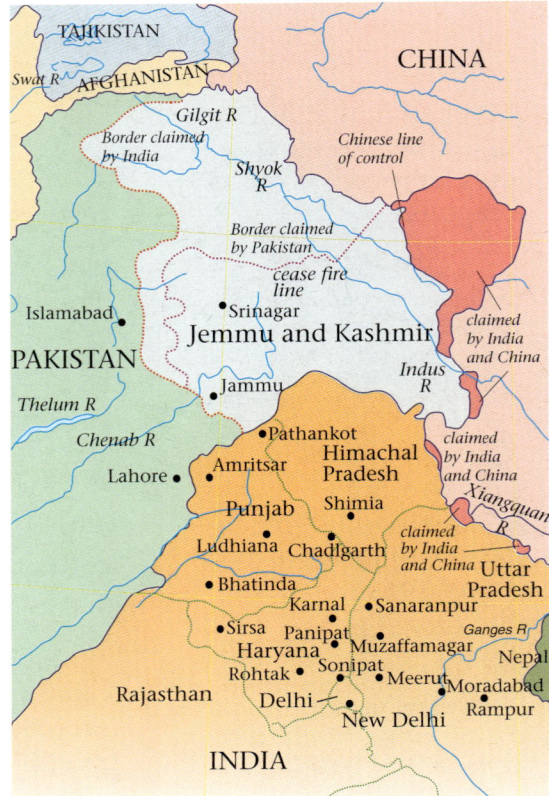

FACTFILE 21

CHRISTIANITY AND WAR

> Blessed are the peacemakers, for they will be called sons of God.

Matthew 5:9

> I tell you, do not resist an evil person. If someone strikes you on the right cheek, turn to him the other also.

Matthew 5:39

> You have heard that it was said, 'Love your neighbour and hate your enemy.' But I tell you: Love your enemies and pray for those who persecute you.

Matthew 5:43–44

> Christians cannot be soldiers because Jesus banned the use of weapons.

Tertullian, a second-century Christian thinker.

> It is wrong for Christians to fight in wars or to have weapons of any kind.

A Declaration from the Harmless and Innocent People of God called Quakers presented to King Charles II.

All Christians believe they should be working for peace because Jesus came to bring peace to the world and Jesus said that those working for peace would be called sons of God. However, there are different attitudes to war among Christians.

1 Christian Pacifism

Some Christians believe that war is so wrong that Christians should never fight in wars. They are called pacifists. There are many Christian pacifist groups such as the Roman Catholic Pax Christi. The Quakers, the Plymouth Brethren and the Christadelphians are churches whose members have to be pacifists.

This memorial for those who suffered for the right to refuse to fight in wars (conscientious objectors) is in the Peace Garden, Tavistock Square, London.

Christian pacifists believe they should not fight because:

- Jesus said Christians should love their enemies and turn the other cheek when attacked;
- The fifth commandment says, 'Do not kill';
- Jesus would not let Peter fight back when Jesus was being arrested;
- horrible things happen to innocent civilians in modern wars;
- they believe that peace can only come when people refuse to fight.

54

2 Christians and the Just War

Most Christian Churches believe that fighting wars can be the best way of bringing peace as long as the war is a just one. A just war is one which:

- is fought in self-defence against an attacker or to remove great unfairness;
- is only fought after all ways of trying to solve the problem without war have been tried;
- uses fair methods;
- does not harm civilians.

This would justify fighting in wars such as Bosnia, Kosovo and Afghanistan.

Austrian soldiers behind the Russian Front, 1916. The Austrian invasion of Serbia began the First World War.

> He (Jesus) said to them, 'But now if you have a purse, take it, and also a bag; and if you don't have a sword, sell your cloak and buy one.'
>
> *Luke 22:36*

> Christians serving in the armed forces of democracies are like a police force, so Christians can regard it as an honour and a duty to serve in the armed forces.

From *Christians and War* published by the Officers' Christian Union.

> Everyone must submit himself to the governing authorities, for there is no authority except that which God has established. The authorities that exist have been established by God.
>
> *Romans 13:1*

Most Christians believe in fighting just wars because:

- St Augustine and St Thomas Aquinas said Christians could fight in just wars (in self-defence against an aggressor or to remove a great injustice);
- Jesus did not condemn soldiers, he actually praised the faith of a Roman centurion;
- St Paul said Christians should obey the orders of the state;
- if we need a police force to protect innocent people against criminals, we need armed forces to protect innocent states against criminal ones.

> If there is a danger of war, countries have a right to defend themselves after trying to make peace.

Catechism of the Catholic Church.

FACTFILE 22

ISLAM AND WAR

Peace is the ideal for all Muslims as one of the meanings of the word Islam is 'peace'. However, Muslims must struggle to make themselves and the world Muslim. The word for struggle is jihad which is often translated as holy war. Islam teaches that it is right for Muslims to fight in a war:

- if Islam is being attacked or if people are suffering injustice;
- if war is the last resort when all other options have been tried to solve the problem;
- if the war is fought in a just way so that the minimum amount of suffering is caused and innocent civilians are not involved.

Muslims believe that this type of war is a struggle for God (jihad) because:

- the Qur'an says that Muslims must fight if they are attacked;
- Muhammad fought in wars;
- there are many hadith from Muhammad saying Muslims should fight in just wars;
- the Qur'an says that Muslims dying in jihad will go straight to heaven.

> Fight in the cause of God those who fight you, but do not transgress the limits; for God loveth not the transgressors.

Surah 2:190

> Think not of those who are slain in God's way as dead. Nay, they live, finding their sustenance in the presence of the Lord.

Surah 3:169

> Muhammad said, 'War is a deception.'

Hadith quoted by Bukhari and Muslim.

> Islam is not in favour of wars. When Muslims meet, they say, 'Salaam aleikum' (which means, 'May peace be with you') instead of, 'Hello.'

Ruqaiyyah Maqsood, *Teach Yourself Islam*.

> Muhammad said, 'Fight for the religion of Allah, but do not kill the old, the young or women.'

Hadith quoted by Abu Daud.

Muslims often protest against unjust wars.

FACTFILE 23

JUDAISM AND WAR

Not all Jews approve of Israel's attitude to war.

Peace is the ideal for all Jews. The Jewish word for 'hello' is 'peace be with you'. However, Judaism expects Jews to fight in a war:

- if God commands it;
- if they are attacked by an enemy;
- if they are asked to aid a country which is being attacked;
- if all other attempts to resolve the conflict have failed.

Jews believe they can fight in wars because:

- there are mitzvot saying that Jews must fight when attacked;
- there are many accounts in the Tenakh of how Israel had to fight wars to preserve her independence;
- the Holocaust reminds Jews what can happen if there is no army to defend Jews against attack.

However, there are some Jewish pacifists who believe that war is wrong in the modern world because modern weapons are bound to harm so many innocent people.

> **If your enemy is hungry, give him food to eat; if he is thirsty, give him water to drink.**
>
> *Proverbs 25:21*

> **Turn from evil and do good; seek peace and pursue it.**
>
> *Psalm 34:14*

> The Torah was given to establish peace.
>
> *Midrash*

> War comes to the world because of a lack of justice.
>
> *Talmud*

> **The law will go out from Zion, the word of the Lord from Jerusalem. He will judge between many peoples and will settle disputes for strong nations far and wide. They will beat their swords into ploughshares and their spears into pruning hooks. Nation will not take up sword against nation, nor will they train for war any more.**
>
> *Micah 4:3*

FACTFILE 24

HINDUISM AND WAR

Although Hinduism is dedicated to peace, there are two different attitudes to war among Hindus.

1 Pacifism and non-violence

Some Hindus believe that violence in any form is wrong and that Hindus should be able to struggle for justice without going to war. They believe this because:

- the Hindu belief of ahimsa means non-violence;
- killing people puts a person's soul further from moksha;
- Gandhi's struggle for Indian independence from the British showed pacifism can work as a way of removing injustice.

2 The Hindu Just War

Many Hindus believe that it is right to fight in wars to resist attack or to remove great injustice. They believe this because:

- the second Hindu caste is the warrior caste whose duty (karma) is to defend Hinduism;
- the Gita says that Hindus must fight in just wars as killing people does not kill their souls;
- there are many stories in the Hindu Scriptures of Hindu gods being involved in wars when they came to earth.

> Prepare for war with peace in thy soul. Be in peace in pleasure and pain, in gain and in loss, in victory or in the loss of a battle. In this peace there is no sin.

Bhagavad Gita 2:38

> Non-violence is not something Hindus can choose, it is an essential part of Hinduism.

Gandhi

Gandhi refused to use violence.

> Non-violence is a weapon which allows even children, women and old men to resist successfully.

Gandhi

> Think thou also of thy duty and do not waver. There is no greater good for a warrior than to fight in a righteous war. There is war that opens up the gates of heaven, Arjuna! Happy the warrior whose fate is to fight such a war.

Bhagavad Gita 2:31–32

Hindu soldiers use the teachings of the Gita to justify fighting in war.

FACTFILE 25

A RELIGIOUS GROUP WORKING FOR WORLD PEACE

Pax Christi is a Roman Catholic group dedicated to peace and non-violence. Pax Christi USA is the American branch. It was founded in 1972 to witness to the call of Christians to non-violence.

The work of Pax Christi

- publicly condemning such things as the NATO bombing of Serbia;
- organising public debates on the morality of nuclear weapons;
- criticising the American Government's defence policy;
- working to remove the causes of war.

Reasons why Pax Christi does the work:

- Jesus said Christians should love their enemies and turn the other cheek when attacked;
- The fifth commandment says, 'Do not kill';
- Jesus would not let Peter fight back when Jesus was being arrested;
- horrible things happen to innocent civilians in modern wars;
- they believe Catholics should be non-violent.

Many Christians think the West is wrong to keep bombing Iraq.

Pax Christi USA is trying to make a world that shows the peace of Christ. Pax Christi USA rejects war and violence and is dedicated to social justice and respect for God's creation.

The Pax Christi statement of purpose to which all members have to agree.

75 US Catholic Bishops Condemn Policy of Nuclear Deterrence

We come to you, compassionate God, carrying in our hearts men and women who need your gifts of love, wisdom and courage: Bill Clinton, Saddam Hussein and their associates who help them make decisions. Give them hearts to listen to the cries of the poor. Help us to respond to violence in the way we have been shown by Jesus.

Part of a Pax Christi prayer for peace.

FACTFILE 26
BULLYING

Bullying takes place at work as well as school. It occurs when stronger people pick on weaker people to make their life a misery and leads to stress, nervous breakdown and even death.

> **Do not defraud your neighbour or rob him. Do not hold back the wages of a hired man overnight. Do not curse the deaf or put a stumbling block in front of the blind, but fear your God, I am the Lord ... Do not go about spreading slander among your people. Do not do anything that endangers your neighbour's life. I am the Lord.**
>
> Leviticus 19:13–16

Religious attitudes to bullying

All religions see bullying as wrong because:

- it is an unjustified use of force, condemned by all religions;
- bullying does not treat people as important individuals which religion says they are;
- religious people should protect the innocent not bully them;

The quotations in the green boxes also show why religious people are against bullying.

Non-religious attitudes to bullying

Society disapproves of bullying and the law protects people from bullying by treating it as a criminal offence and making all schools have an anti-bullying policy which all pupils have to be told about.

Non-religious people are against bullying because:

- it denies people's human rights;
- it prevents people from making their contribution to society;
- it threatens the rule of law on which society depends.

> **This is the message you heard from the beginning: We should love one another. Do not be like Cain who belonged to the evil one and murdered his brother. And why did he murder him? Because his own actions were evil and his brother's were righteous... Anyone who hates his brother is a murderer, and you know that no murderer has eternal life in him.**
>
> 1 John 3:11–15

BLUNKETT ACTS TO ELIMINATE BULLYING

David Blunkett urged schoolchildren not to 'suffer in silence' yesterday as he unveiled advice to schools on how to stop bullying.

In the new guidance, the Education Secretary encouraged head teachers to set up 'peer mentoring' schemes where children acted as counsellors to younger children and urged them not to ignore bullying outside the school gates.

It is believed that up to a million children a year are bullied with up to a third of girls and a quarter of boys afraid to go to school as a result. About ten cases each year end in suicide. Damilola Taylor, the ten-year-old boy who died after complaining of bullying at school in Peckham, has recently brought the issue to light.

The Times, 14 December 2000.

David Blunkett, the Minister of Education, set up measures to stop bullying in schools.

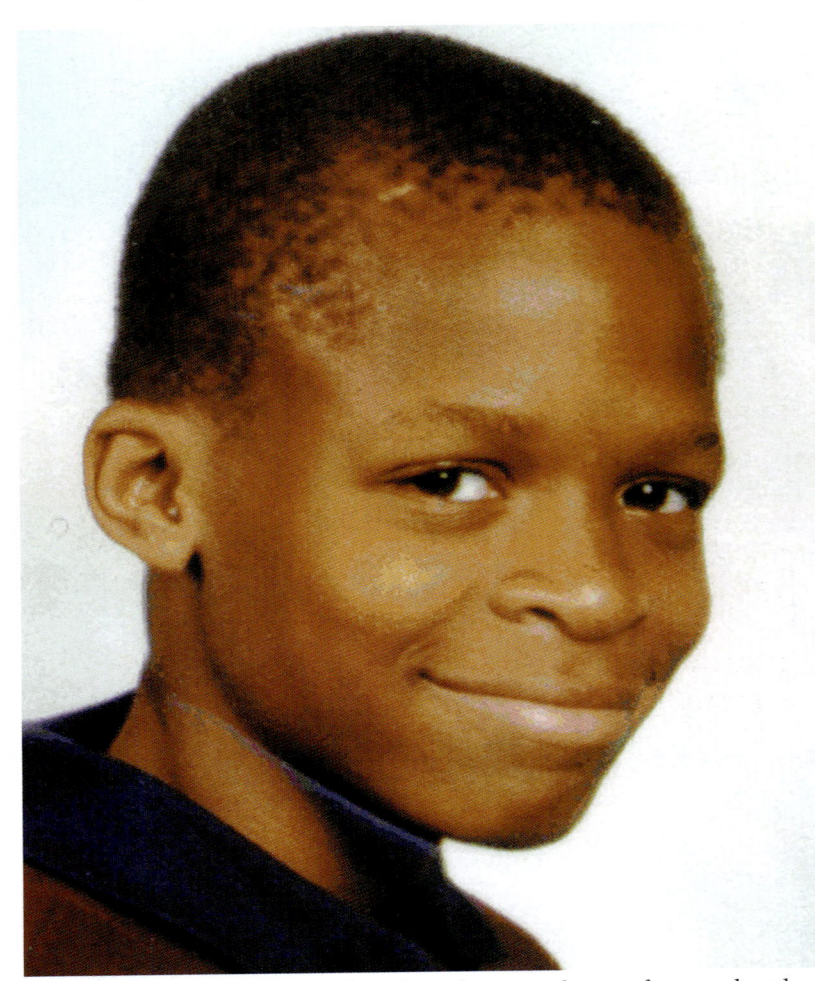

Damilola Taylor was murdered on his way home from school.

> Let there arise out of you a band of people inviting to all that is good, enjoining what is right, and forbidding what is wrong: they are the one to attain felicity. Be not like those who are divided among themselves and fall into disputations after receiving clear signs: for them is a dreadful penalty.

Qur'an 3: 104–105

> The principle of ahimsa does not include any evil thought, any unjustified haste, any lies, hatred, ill-will towards anyone.

Mahatma Gandhi

FACTFILE 27

CAUSES OF CONFLICT BETWEEN FAMILIES AND FRIENDS

Family strife began in Coronation Street when a father began an affair.

For most people the most worrying conflicts are those that occur between friends or among families. They can happen for many reasons:

- jealousy of success e.g. when a friend wins the lottery or a relative is given a very good job;
- parents refusing to accept their children's choice of partner;
- disagreements among children over the care of aged parents;
- disagreements over the content of wills;
- disagreements over moral issues.

Religion says that the best way to deal with such conflicts is forgiveness.

Neighbours go to court over hedge

Young wife only married for money say children contesting will

Who Wants to be a Millionaire winner refuses to reward friend whose answer made £250,000

Parents refuse to attend daughter's wedding to African

Christians believe that it is their duty to try to bring together families and friends who are in conflict (reconciliation) and that it is a Christian's duty to forgive those who attack them. They believe this because:

- Jesus died on the cross to bring reconciliation and forgiveness;
- Jesus told Peter to forgive people up to seventy-seven times;
- Jesus said that if Christians do not forgive others, they will not be forgiven themselves;
- St Paul said that Christians should try to live in peace with everyone.

Nevertheless, Christians believe that a conflict about a moral or religious issue would not be able to be resolved for example, if parents argued that a Roman Catholic son should not become a priest.

The Crucifixion by Craigie Aitchison (1959).

FACTFILE 28

CHRISTIANITY AND FORGIVENESS

> Then Peter came to Jesus and asked, 'Lord, how many times shall I forgive my brother when he sins against me? Up to seven times?' Jesus answered, 'I tell you not seven times, but seventy-seven times.'

Matthew 18:21–22

> And when you stand praying, if you hold anything against anyone, forgive him, so that your Father in heaven may forgive you your sins.

Mark 11:26

> If anyone has caused grief ... you ought to forgive and comfort him.

2 Corinthians 2:7

> Forgiveness shows that love is stronger than sin. Forgiveness is the only way to bring reconciliation between humans and between humans and God.

Catechism of the Catholic Church.

FACTFILE 29

ISLAM AND FORGIVENESS

Islam teaches that Muslims should try to resolve conflicts and should be forgiving to those who cause them offence. They believe this because:

- God is Compassionate and Merciful to sinners, so Muslims should also be forgiving;
- how can Muslims ask for God's forgiveness on the Last Day if they are not prepared to forgive people?
- the Qur'an says that Muslims should forgive those who offend them;
- Muhammad said in many hadiths that Muslims should be forgiving.

Nevertheless, Muslims believe that a conflict over moral or religious issues would not be able to be resolved for example, if Muslims were drinking alcohol or gambling.

> The recompense for an injury is an injury equal thereto in degree; but if a person forgives and makes reconciliation, his reward is due from God.

Surah 42:40

> If anyone does evil or wrongs his own soul, but afterwards seeks God's forgiveness, he will find God Oft-forgiving, Most Merciful.

Surah 4:110

> Be forgiving and control yourself in the face of provocation; give justice to the person who was unfair and unjust to you; give to the one who did not help you when you were in need, and keep fellowship with the one who did not care about you.

Hadith

> A kind word with forgiveness is better than charity followed by injury.

Surah 2:263

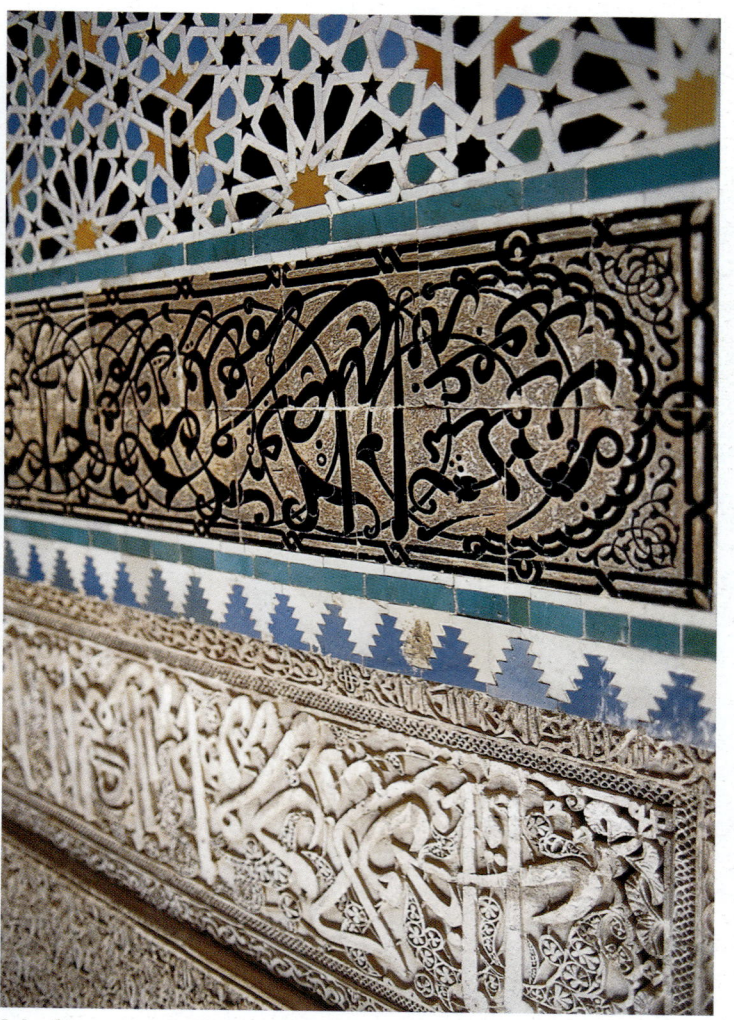

Muslims use calligraphy as decoration and it often reminds them that Allah is Compassionate and Merciful.

FACTFILE 30

JUDAISM AND FORGIVENESS

> So they sent word to Joseph saying, 'Your father left these instructions before he died: "This is what you are to say to Joseph: I ask you to forgive your brothers the sins and wrongs they committed in treating you so badly."'

Genesis 50:16–17

> You are forgiving and good, O Lord, abounding in love to all who call to you.

Psalm 86:5

The Yom Kippur service encourages forgiveness.

Judaism teaches that Jews should forgive those who wrong them. Jews believe in forgiveness because:

- the Tenakh teaches that God forgives those who turn to him in repentance;
- the Tenakh teaches that Jews should forgive those who wrong them;
- Rabbis encourage Jews to forgive those who wrong them;
- it is Jewish belief that Jews should forgive those who have wronged them when on their deathbed so that God will forgive their sins;
- in the days between Rosh Hashanah and Yom Kippur, Jews have to settle any quarrels they have had with families or friends over the past year.

Nevertheless, Jews believe that a conflict over moral or religious issues would not be able to be resolved for example, if a son or daughter began to eat pork.

> Judaism says that God cannot forgive you if you have not forgiven other people.

Judaism, C. M. Pilkington.

> And so, may it be your will, Lord our God, to have mercy on us and forgive us all our sins.

From the prayers for Yom Kippur.

67

FACTFILE 31

HINDUISM AND FORGIVENESS

There are differences among Hindus in their attitudes to forgiveness.

> When a man sees all beings within his very self, and his self within all beings ... he has reached the seed – without body or wound, without sinews, not riddled by evil.

Isa Upanishad 6–8

> Even if someone attacks you with abuses, insults and beatings for no reason, do not be harsh to them. Bear and endure them. Forgive and bless your tormentors.

Shiksapatri 202

> According as one acts, according as one conducts oneself, so does one become. The doer of good becomes good. The doer of evil becomes evil. One becomes virtuous by virtuous action, bad by bad action.

Brhadaranyaka Upanishad 4.4.5

Hindu swamis encourage forgiveness of others to free the soul.

Some Hindus do not believe in forgiveness because:
- they believe that everything is a result of karma and nothing should be done to change people's karma.

Most Hindus believe in forgiveness because:
- it is better for one's soul to forgive those who have committed wrong;
- in the gunas, forgiveness is a quality of light which leads the soul to moksha;
- the Upanishads teach that it is dangerous for the soul not to forgive;
- many swamis believe that forgiveness is a part of moksha.

QUESTIONS

Factfile 20 War and peace issues

1 Name two weapons of mass destruction.
2 Choose one area of conflict in the world today and give three reasons why the conflict is happening.

Factfile 21 Christianity and war

1 What is pacifism?
2 Give three reasons why some Christians are pacifists.
3 Give three reasons why some Christians believe they can fight in just wars.

Factfile 22, 23, 24 Islam, Judaism and Hinduism and war

1 Choose one religion other than Christianity and outline its attitude to war.
2 'It is an insult to God to spend billions on weapons when people are starving.'
   a) Give two reasons for agreeing with this statement.
   b) Give two reasons for disagreeing with this statement.

Factfile 25 A religious group working for world peace

Give an outline of the work of one religious group working for world peace.

Factfile 26 Bullying

1 State three effects of bullying.
2 Have a class discussion on how bullying can be prevented.

Factfile 27 Causes of conflict between family and friends

1 What are the main causes of conflict between families?
2 What are the main causes of conflict between friends?

Factfile 28 Christianity and forgiveness

Give an outline of Christian teaching on forgiveness.

Factfile 29, 30, 31 Islam, Judaism and Hinduism and forgiveness

1 Choose one religion other than Christianity and give an outline of its teachings on forgiveness.
2 'Religious people should never argue with their families.'
   a) Give two reasons for agreeing with this statement.
   b) Give two reasons for disagreeing with this statement.

4 CRIME AND PUNISHMENT

Sin – an act against the will of God.

Crime – an act against the law.

Law – rules made by Parliament and enforceable by the courts.

Justice – due allocation of reward and punishment, the maintenance of what is right.

Deterrence – the idea that punishments should be of such a nature that they will put people off (deter) committing crimes.

Retribution – the idea that punishments should make criminals pay for what they have done wrong.

Reform – the idea that punishments should try to change criminals so they will not commit crimes again.

Judgement – the act of judging people and their actions.

Punishment – a penalty given for any crime or offence.

Capital punishment – the death penalty for a crime or offence.

FACTFILE 32

LAW AND JUSTICE

Laws are rules about how to behave.

Justice is about making sure that what is right happens in society and that the good are rewarded and the evil punished.

A sin is an act against the will of God, for example rich people refusing to share with the poor.

A crime is an act against the law, for example Martin Luther King sitting on a bus seat reserved for white people.

Sins are not always crimes and crimes are not always sins which means that there can be laws which are not just. It is important for laws to be just so that people feel it is right to obey them.

Christian leaders such as Martin Luther King encourage Christians to challenge the law if it is unjust.

Why do we need laws?

Humans live in societies and societies use laws to organise things. Without laws, life would be terrible. Imagine what life would be like if there were no laws on stealing, murder, rape ...

Society needs laws because:

- people need to know how other people will behave;
- people need to be sure that what they make from their work will not be stolen from them or else they will not bother to work;
- people need to be protected from violence.

Why does there need to be a connection between the law and justice?

If laws do not make sure that what is right happens, and that the good are rewarded and the evil punished, then people will start to break the law.

The Old Bailey is the most famous Crown Court in the United Kingdom.

> Continual fear and danger of violent death; and the life of man solitary, poor, nasty, brutish and short.

Thomas Hobbes saying what life would be like without laws in his book *Leviathan*.

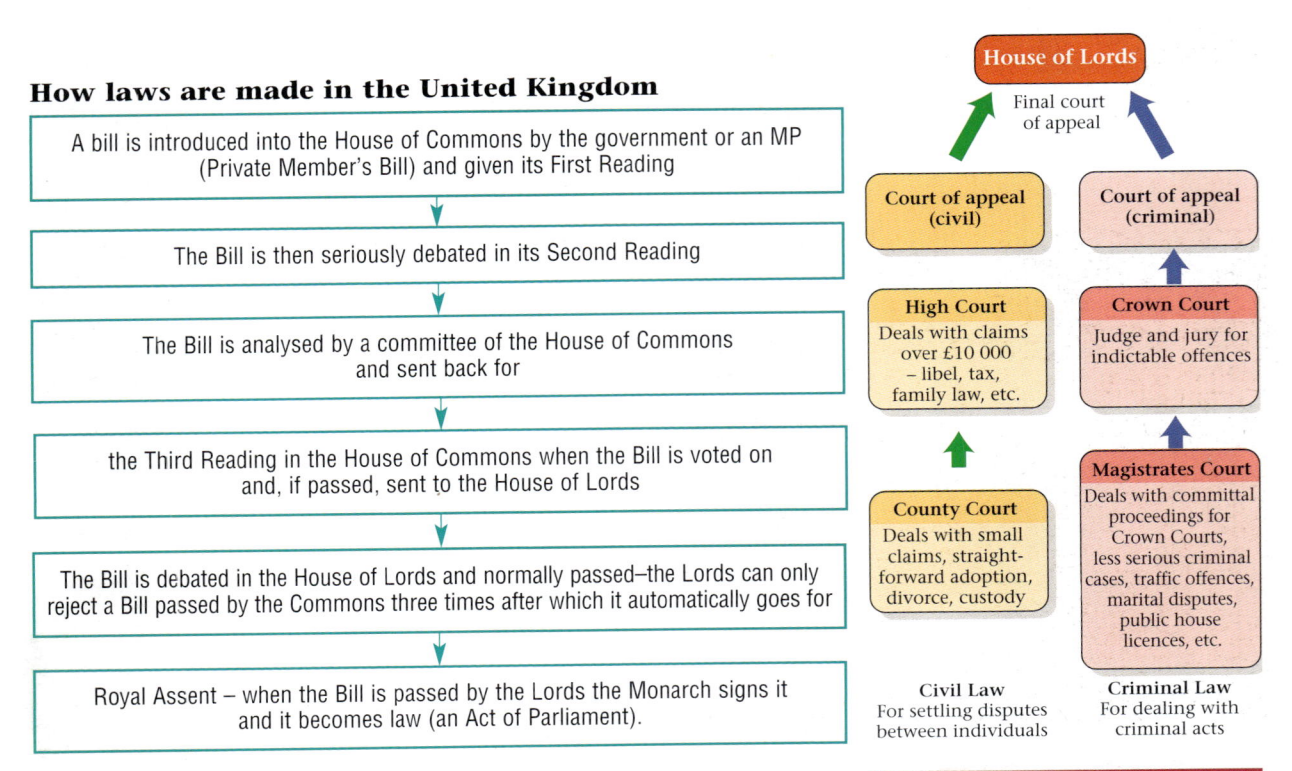

How laws are made in the United Kingdom

- A bill is introduced into the House of Commons by the government or an MP (Private Member's Bill) and given its First Reading
- The Bill is then seriously debated in its Second Reading
- The Bill is analysed by a committee of the House of Commons and sent back for
- the Third Reading in the House of Commons when the Bill is voted on and, if passed, sent to the House of Lords
- The Bill is debated in the House of Lords and normally passed—the Lords can only reject a Bill passed by the Commons three times after which it automatically goes for
- Royal Assent – when the Bill is passed by the Lords the Monarch signs it and it becomes law (an Act of Parliament).

House of Lords — Final court of appeal

Court of appeal (civil)

High Court — Deals with claims over £10 000 – libel, tax, family law, etc.

County Court — Deals with small claims, straight-forward adoption, divorce, custody

Civil Law — For settling disputes between individuals

Court of appeal (criminal)

Crown Court — Judge and jury for indictable offences

Magistrates Court — Deals with committal proceedings for Crown Courts, less serious criminal cases, traffic offences, marital disputes, public house licences, etc.

Criminal Law — For dealing with criminal acts

FACTFILE 33

CHRISTIANITY AND JUSTICE

Christians believe that the world should be ruled justly and that God will reward the good and punish the bad. They believe that they should work for justice and so they:

- campaign for the cancelling of Third World debt (Jubilee 2000);
- work to improve life in LDCs (e.g. Christian Aid);
- work for poor people in the UK (e.g. the Salvation Army).

The Chapel of Justice in Exeter Cathedral is a sign of the importance of justice in Christianity. It encourages Christians to pray for justice in the world and organises events for groups such as: the Devon Forum for Justice, Christian Aid, The Devon Christian Ecology Group, and the Devon HIV/AIDS Association.

> **And there is no God apart from me, a just God and a saviour.**
>
> *Isaiah 45:21*

> **Blessed are those who hunger and thirst for righteousness.**
>
> *Matthew 5:6*

> **Anyone who does not do what is right (just) is not a child of God; nor is anyone who does not love his brother.**
>
> *1 John 3:10*

The Chapel of Justice in Exeter Cathedral.

Christians believe in justice because:

- the Bible shows God is a God of justice;
- the Bible says people should be treated fairly;
- Jesus said that the rich should share with the poor;
- there are many statements in the New Testament about sharing with the poor;
- the Churches have made statements about the need for Christians to work for justice in the world.

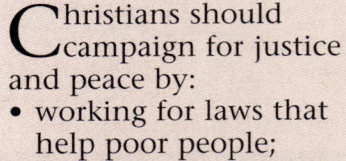

Christians should campaign for justice and peace by:
- working for laws that help poor people;
- trying to help world hunger;
- working with people from other faiths and cultures;
- working for disarmament.

From a pamphlet of the Exeter Diocesan Board for Christian Care.

Inside the Chapel of Justice.

Thank you God for the freedom to raise my voice in protest. Thank you God that I can stand with poor people and make a difference.

Christian Aid prayer.

FACTFILE 34

ISLAM AND JUSTICE

Muslims believe that the world should be ruled justly and that God will reward the good and punish the bad. Muslims believe it is part of their role as God's khalifah to make sure that the world is governed in a fair way. So they believe that the laws of the world should be the law of God (Shari'ah).

> O ye who believe! Stand out firmly for justice, as witnesses to God, even as against yourselves or your parents, or your kin, and whether it be against rich or poor.

Surah 4:135

ISLAMIC INVESTMENT BANKING UNIT

Serving the Muslim community today...and even better tomorrow.

Islamic Investment Banking Unit
7 Baker Street,
London W1M 1AB

The Islamic Investment Banking Unit is here for you. For some time now we've been offering financial assistance to Muslims who wish to buy homes in a way that complies with Islamic Sharia'a.

Our Manzil Home Purchase Plans have proved a very popular choice.

But this is just the start.

We're working to introduce many more products especially designed for you. Our goal is to give Muslims in the U.K. the opportunity to conduct all their financial affairs in a manner consistent with their faith. Insha'Allah, you'll be hearing much more from us in the year to come.

For more information, please contact Waheed Qaiser, Head of UK Islamic Business on our freephone number **0800 783 3323**
Or visit our new website at **www.iibu.com**

Written information about the terms on which IIBU is prepared to do business in relation to Manzil for a specific transaction are available on request. Your home is at risk if you do not keep up your repayments on a mortgage, other loan or facility secured on it. IIBU is a segregated division of The United Bank of Kuwait PLC, British bank regulated by the Financial Services Authority (FSA) and Investment Management Regulatory Organisation (IMRO).

> Say, 'My Lord hath commanded justice.'

Surah 7:29

> And the firmament has He raised high, and He has set up the balance of justice in order that ye may not transgress.

Surah 55:7

Muslims believe that all people should have equal rights and as part of their belief in justice they work for a fairer share of resources for LDCs through:

- groups like Muslim Aid,
- the pillar of zakah,
- refusing to be involved in the charging of interest.

Ramadan Appeal

Even during this holy month millions of men, women and children around the world are without basic necessities - food, water, medicines and shelter.

Your donation today can go a long way in helping alleviate their suffering.

Muslim Aid

PO Box 3 ♦ London N7 8LR ♦ Telephone 0171-609 4425

My Ramadan gift for those in need... RL2

☐ Zakah £ _____   ☐ Zakatul Fitr @ £3/head £ _____
☐ Sadaqah £ _____   ☐ (Other fund - please specify) £ _____
☐ I enclose cheque (made payable to Muslim Aid) for £ _____
Mr/Mrs/Miss
Address
Postcode   Telephone
Please post to: Muslim Aid, P O Box 3, London N7 8LR

Regd Charity No 295224

Muslims believe this because:

- the Qur'an says God is just;
- the Qur'an says that Muslims should treat people fairly;
- Muslims believe it is part of their role as vice-gerents of God's creation to treat all people fairly;
- the Shari'ah is based on justice for everyone with everyone being treated equally.

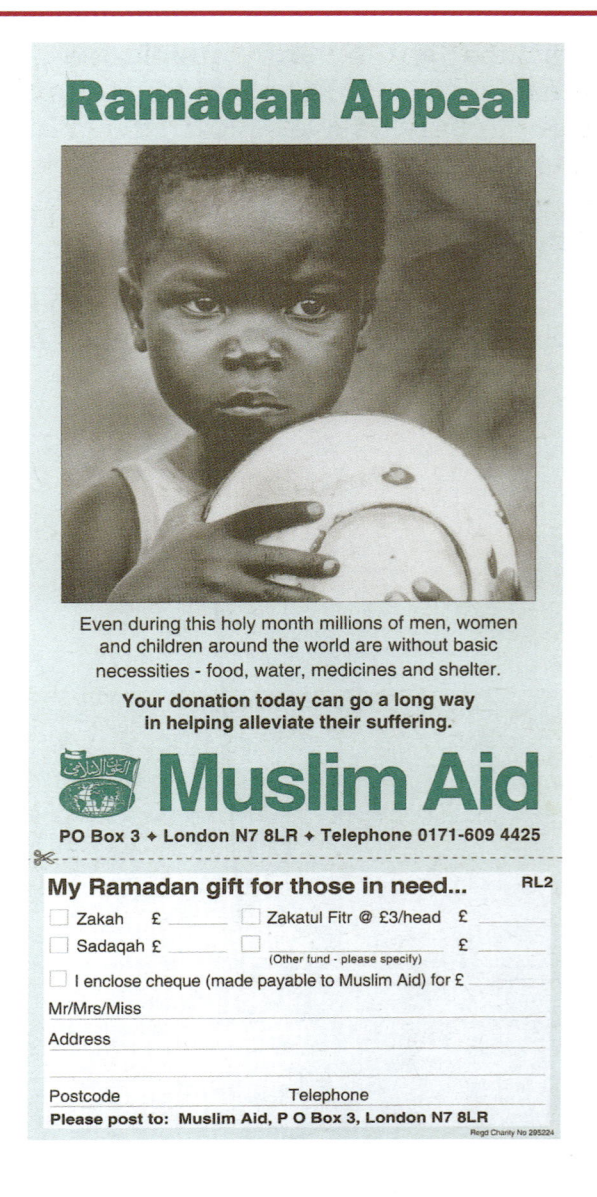

> Boraidah reported that the Prophet said: Judges are of three kinds: One kind will be in Paradise and two in Hell. As for one who will be in Paradise, he is a man who recognises truth and gives a decree accordingly, and a man who recognises truth but is unjust in decree is in Hell, and a man who passes a decree for the people out of ignorance is in Hell.

Hadith quoted by Abu Daud.

> Everyone should be equal in Islamic justice. There must be no different treatment of rich and poor, Muslim and non-Muslim.

Nisar Ahmed, *The Fundamental Teachings of Qur'an and Hadith*.

> Zakah bridges the gulf between rich and poor, providing economic security for the whole of society and giving Muslims the chance to work for social justice.

Islamic Relief Zakat Guide.

FACTFILE 35

JUDAISM AND JUSTICE

Jews believe that justice is very important and that God wants the world to be ruled justly. They believe that all people should have equal rights. As part of their belief in justice:

- many Jews have been involved in campaigns for equal rights for black people;
- Jews work for a fairer sharing of the earth's resources not only by helping World Jewish Relief, but also groups such as Oxfam.

> Oh, praise the greatness of our God! He is the Rock, his works are perfect and all his ways are just. A faithful God who does no wrong, upright and just is he.

Deuteronomy 32:3–4

Anatole Scharansky, a leading scientist who campaigned for equal rights for Jews in the USSR.

They believe this because:

- the Torah says that God is a God of Justice;
- the Tenakh says that all people should be treated fairly;
- the Tenakh, Talmud and rabbis say that the rich should share with the poor;
- there are many statements in the Responsa about how Jews should treat all people fairly and equally.

World Jewish Relief sends medical and food aid to bring justice to the people of Bosnia.

> Seek good, not evil, that you may live. Then the Lord God almighty will be with you, just as you say he is. Hate evil, love good; maintain justice in the courts.

Amos 5:14–15

> The worst way of giving to charity is to give it sadly. A better way is to give before being asked. The best way is to take the poor into business or help them to be independent.

Jewish Values – Maimonides.

> Without laws people would tear each other apart.

Ethics of the Fathers.

> The Talmud tells the story of a Jewish rabbi who refused to be judged in a trial because the accused had helped him into a boat.

Adapted from the *Talmud*.

77

FACTFILE 36

HINDUISM AND JUSTICE

> Who have all the powers of their soul in harmony, and the same loving mind for all; who find joy in the good of all beings – they reach in truth my very self.

Bhagavad Gita 12:4

> May all be righteous and without suffering.

Hindu prayer.

> The Law of Manu states quite clearly that unjust actions such as theft, violence, adultery, lying, slander and gossip will bring retribution in a future life.

Themes and Issues in Hinduism, P Bowen.

> If you are a leader of the state, you must treat your subjects as your family and try to bring justice.

Shikshapatri of Lord Swaminarayan.

The Hindu idea of justice is based on dharma. For most Hindus this means that they should try to make the world a place of justice. Mahatma Gandhi based his campaign for Indian independence from British rule on the Hindu idea of justice.

Hindus work for justice by:
- treating all people as equals;
- working for equal rights;
- working for a fairer sharing of the earth's resources.

Hindus are concerned to bring justice to all the people of India.

Hindus believe in justice because:
- the Hindu goal is to gain moksha and this means fulfilling the dharma and working for justice;
- the Hindu scriptures encourage Hindus to work for justice;
- great Hindu leaders such as Gandhi spent their lives working for justice;
- Hindu gurus and swamis teach that treating people justly improves the soul.

Some Hindus believe that justice comes through operating the caste system correctly. They believe this because:
- the caste system rewards the good for what they did in their past lives;
- the caste system punishes the bad for what they did in their past lives.

FACTFILE 37

THE NATURE OF PUNISHMENT

Many people think prisons should treat criminals very harshly to make people frightened of being sent to prison.

To make sure that laws are obeyed and there is justice in society, there needs to be a police force and a court system to stop people breaking the law and to punish those who break the law.

The main aim of punishment is to make people obey the law, but there are several theories of punishment:

- **retribution** – the idea that criminals should pay for their crimes;
- **deterrence** – the idea that if punishments are severe enough, people will be frightened of committing crimes;
- **reform** – the idea that people who commit crimes need to be shown why it is wrong and helped to lead crime-free lives;
- **protection** – the idea that punishment should be used to protect society from criminals who cannot be reformed.

Most forms of punishment are a mixture of ideas, for example prison protects, deters, reforms and gives retribution.

Drug Dealer freed for saving man

A convicted drugs dealer has had 14 days removed from his 30-month prison sentence for saving a motorcyclist's life. The prisoner was on his way to hospital when prison officers stopped at a road accident and allowed him to use the first aid skills he had learnt in prison to stop the man from bleeding to death.

The Times, 8 November 2000.

I have probably seen 350 young people come through the secure unit and all of them have had an experience which led them to crime. One boy was made to live in a kennel, another had bleach poured over him to make him white. Many of them have never had their teeth cleaned. People don't know what young criminals have been through.

Statement from the head of education in a secure unit for young offenders which tries to reform young teenagers who have committed very serious crimes.

FACTFILE 38

CHRISTIANITY AND PUNISHMENT

There are two different attitudes to punishment among Christians.

1 Some Christians believe that the only purpose of punishment is to reform the criminal. Everyone can be saved and criminals should be given the chance to repent and change their lives.

They believe this because:

- Jesus said Christians should not judge others;
- Christianity is about the power of God to save people and change their lives;
- the Church has always seen itself as a way to bring new life to criminals;
- the Churches have made many statements about the need for punishment to be used to reform criminals so that they can live in society.

> Do not judge or you too will be judged. For in the same way as you judge others, you will be judged.

Matthew 7:1–2

> 'If any one of you is without sin, let him be the first to throw a stone at her.' ... At this, those who heard began to go away ...
>
> Jesus straightened up and asked her, 'Woman where are they? Has no one condemned you?'
>
> 'No one sir,' she said.
>
> 'Then neither do I condemn you,' Jesus declared.

John 8:7–11

The sanctuary knocker at Durham Cathedral dates from the Middle Ages when the Bishop allowed criminals who touched the knocker to leave the country.

2 Some Christians believe that punishment should be used to deter criminals and to protect society as well as reforming them.

They believe this because:
- St Paul said magistrates should uphold the law;
- without a police force and punishment for criminals society would collapse;
- the Churches have made statements that punishment can be used to deter and protect;
- Jesus punished the money changers when he threw them out of the Temple.

> I urge then, first of all, that prayers and intercessions be made for everyone – for kings and all those in authority, that we may live peaceful and quiet lives in all godliness and holiness.

1 Timothy 2:1–2

> But I tell you, do not resist an evil person. If someone strikes you on the right cheek, turn to him the other also.

Matthew 5:39

Anne Widdecombe is a Christian politician who thinks punishment should be based on deterrence and retribution.

> Christians realise that the Government has a duty to protect society by punishing criminals, but the aim of punishment should be to reform offenders.

Statement by the Methodist Church in *What the Churches Say* second edition.

> The Salvation Army recognises that society needs to be protected from violent wrongdoers, but punishments should treat criminals as human beings and try to reform them.

Statement by the Salvation Army on punishment quoted in *What the Churches Say* second edition.

FACTFILE 39

ISLAM AND PUNISHMENT

Islam teaches that punishment should be based on deterrence and reform. Severe punishments are used to make people afraid of committing crimes. Some crimes are punished by retribution where the criminal pays compensation to the victim or the victim's family.

> As to the thief, male or female, cut off his or her hands: a punishment by way of example, from God, for their crime.

Surah 5:41

> The recompense for an injury is an injury equal thereto in degree: but if a person forgives and makes retribution, his reward is due from God: for God loveth not those who do wrong.

Surah 42:40

> The woman and the man guilty of adultery and fornication, flog each of them with a hundred stripes: let not compassion move you in their case, in a matter prescribed by God.

Surah 24:2

> Ayesha reported that the Messenger of Allah said: Verily those who were before you were destroyed because when a noble man from them committed theft, they let him off, and when a workman committed theft from among them, they exempted sentence on him. By Allah, had Fatima, daughter of Muhammad, committed theft, I would have cut off her hand.

Hadith reported in all the authorities.

Would Islamic punishments deter all criminals?

Muslims believe that punishment should be based on deterrence, retribution and reform because:

- it is what the Qur'an teaches;
- the Qur'an states that some crimes must be punished by whipping, some by amputation and some by compensation;
- the Shari'ah makes sure that the punishment is only given to the guilty.

FACTFILE 40

JUDAISM AND PUNISHMENT

Jews believe that society has a right to punish criminals. They believe that the reasons for punishment are deterrence, protection and retribution. However, they also see that there should be some reform, as successful reform of criminals is a way of protecting society from future crimes.

They believe this because:

- the Torah says that criminals should be punished;
- the Torah gives deterrence, protection and retribution as the reasons for punishment;
- society would collapse if criminals were not punished;
- rabbis have always been involved in the Jewish court system.

> But if there is serious injury, you are to take life for life, eye for eye, tooth for tooth, hand for hand, foot for foot, burn for burn, wound for wound, bruise for bruise.

Exodus 21:23–24

> While the Israelites were in the desert, a man was found gathering wood on the Sabbath day. Those who found him gathering wood brought him to Moses and Aaron and the whole assembly, and they kept him in custody because it was not clear what should be done to him.

Numbers 15:34

The Bet Din is the court for British Jews on religious matters.

FACTFILE 41

Hinduism and punishment

Hindus believe that it is part of the dharma of rulers to punish those who break the law. Hindus believe that punishment should be used to deter criminals, protect society from criminals, reform criminals so that society is protected from future crime. They also believe in retribution so that criminals pay for what they have done.

Indian courts work on the same principles as British courts.

They believe this because:

- the Vedas and Upanishads say that crimes must be punished;
- other Hindu scriptures give guidelines on punishments;
- the Mahabharata says that a ruler has a duty to punish criminals;
- the law of karma is based on retribution.

FACTFILE 42

Prisoners of Conscience

You have to study a prisoner of conscience (this means someone who has not committed any crimes) who has been imprisoned for their religious beliefs. The prisoner can be from the twentieth or twenty-first centuries.

A prisoner of conscience from the time of the Nazis and the Second World War was Dietrich Bonhoeffer.

Bonhoeffer was a Christian pacifist and a lecturer in Christianity at Berlin University. When Hitler came to power, Bonhoeffer criticised him in radio broadcasts and in lectures. Bonhoeffer was banned from teaching in Germany and became pastor of two German Lutheran churches in London. Whilst in London he tried to tell the British the truth about Hitler.

In 1935, Bonhoeffer returned to Germany to train pastors who were against Hitler and he was arrested in 1937.

Reasons for the arrest

- He had made statements saying that Christians should not obey the Nazi laws on the Jews;
- he said that Christians should refuse to do military service for the Nazis;
- he had preached sermons in Berlin saying that Christians should not obey laws which were against Christian principles.

Hitler was meant to die in the July bomb plot of 1944.

> The leader who makes an idol of himself and his office makes a mockery of God.

Bonhoeffer's radio broadcast in 1933 which was halted by the Nazis.

James Mawdsley's Christian beliefs led to his imprisonment for campaigning for human rights in Burma.

> When the Church sees the state doing wrong, it is its duty to try to stop what the state is doing.

From a Bonhoeffer sermon.

Bonhoeffer's arrest made him realise that pacifism could not work with the Nazis and he decided that it was his Christian duty to join the German movement which was trying to overthrow Hitler and the Nazis.

Bonhoeffer was involved in plots to kill Hitler and after the July Bomb Plot failed in 1944, he was arrested again and executed at Flossenberg extermination camp in April 1945, just before the war ended.

Capital punishment is a punishment which takes away the life of the criminal. It is also called execution or the death penalty. Capital punishment has not been used in the United Kingdom since 1970.

FACTFILE 43

CAPITAL PUNISHMENT

Non-religious arguments in favour of capital punishment

- if people know they will die if they murder someone, they will not murder;
- if murderers are executed, they are no longer a threat to society;
- the only punishment to fit the crime of taking a life is to take the murderer's life.

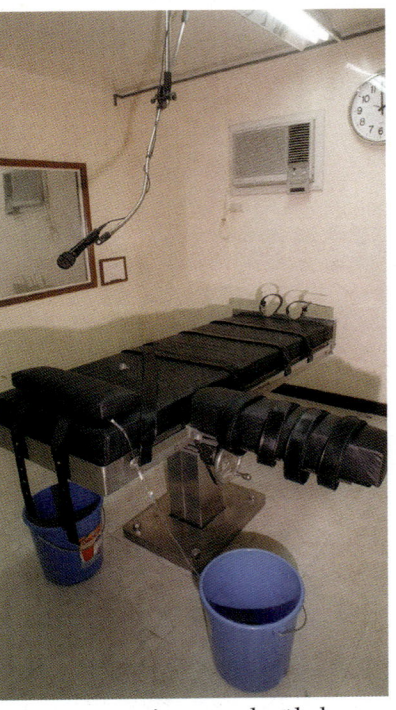

Some countries use death by injection as capital punishment.

Non-religious arguments against capital punishment

- courts do convict innocent people and nothing can be done to release an innocent person who has been executed;
- statistics show that countries who do not use the death penalty have a lower murder rate than those which do;
- murderers do not expect to be caught when they commit their murders;
- murderers try to commit suicide when they are serving life imprisonment, so prison must be a worse sentence than death.

FACTFILE 44

CHRISTIANITY AND CAPITAL PUNISHMENT

> The Laws of the Realm may punish Christian men with death for heinous and grievous offences.

Article 37 of the Thirty Nine Articles of the Church of England.

> You have heard that it was said, 'Eye for eye, tooth for tooth.' But I tell you, Do not resist an evil person. If someone strikes you on the right cheek, turn to him the other also.

Matthew 5:38

10 Rillington Place. Timothy Evans was executed for murders which took place here, but it was later proved that he did not commit them.

Many Christians believe that capital punishment is un-Christian and that Christians should never use capital punishment. They believe this because:

- Jesus came to save (reform) sinners, but you cannot reform a dead person;
- Jesus said that an eye for an eye and a tooth for a tooth is wrong for Christians;
- Christianity teaches that all life is sacred, if abortion and euthanasia are wrong so is capital punishment;
- most Christian Churches have made statements condemning capital punishment;
- they also believe all the non-religious arguments against capital punishment.

Other Christians believe that capital punishment can be used to prevent murder and keep order in society. They believe this because:

- the Old Testament gives the death penalty as the punishment for various offences;
- the Roman Catholic Church and the Church of England have not cancelled their statements that capital punishment can be used by the state;
- Christian thinkers such as St Thomas Aquinas said that the protection of society is a more important part of punishment than the reform of the criminal;
- they would also use all the non-religious arguments in favour of capital punishment.

> If a man hates his neighbour and lies in wait for him, assaults and kills him and then flees to one of these cities, the elders of his town shall send for him, bring him back from the city and hand him over to the avenger of blood to die. Show him no pity. You must purge from Israel the guilt of shedding innocent blood.

Deuteronomy 19:11–13

> We do not have the right to punish murderers by taking their lives. The United Reformed Church believes that even the worst person can be reformed by imprisonment.

Statement by the United Reform Church quoted in *What the Churches Say*, second edition.

> Do not repay anyone evil for evil. Be careful to do what is right in the sight of everybody ... Do not take revenge, my friends, but leave room for God's wrath, for it is written, 'It is mine to revenge, I will repay.'

Romans 12:17–19

FACTFILE 45

ISLAM AND CAPITAL PUNISHMENT

Almost all Muslims agree with capital punishment. They believe this because:

- the Qur'an says that death is the punishment for murder, adultery and denying Islam;
- Muhammad made several statements agreeing with capital punishment;
- Muhammad sentenced people to death when he was ruler of Madinah;
- the Shari'ah says that death is the punishment for murder, adultery and denying Islam;
- they would also agree with all the non-religious arguments in favour of capital punishment.

> Take not life – which God has made sacred – except for just cause.

Surah 17:33

> The shedding of the blood of a Muslim is not lawful except for one of three reasons: a life for a life, a married person who commits adultery and one who turns aside from his religion and abandons the community.

Hadith quoted by Bukhari and Muslim.

Execution is permitted in Muslim States.

A few Muslims disagree with capital punishment because of the non-religious arguments against it.

> In an Islamic country, Islam is the state and so apostasy (giving up Islam) is an act of treason which is punished by death in many countries.

What Does Islam Say? Ibrahim Hewitt.

FACTFILE 46

JUDAISM AND CAPITAL PUNISHMENT

Mass murderers Fred and Rosemary West. He committed suicide rather than serve life imprisonment.

Most Jews agree with capital punishment, but only if there is no possibility of reforming the murderer. They believe this because:

- the Torah says that capital punishment should be used for certain crimes;
- the Talmud says capital punishment can be used but with many restrictions;
- the basis of punishment is the protection of society and so murderers who will always be a danger to society should be executed;
- they would also use the non-religious arguments in favour of capital punishment.

Some Jews do not agree with capital punishment because of the teachings of the Mishnah and the non-religious arguments against capital punishment.

> **If anyone takes the life of a human being, he must be put to death. Anyone who takes the life of someone's animal must make restitution – life for life.**
>
> *Leviticus 24:17*

> **On the testimony of two or three witnesses, a man shall be put to death, but no one shall be put to death on the testimony of only one witness.**
>
> *Deuteronomy 17:6*

> **I believe with perfect faith that the Creator, blessed be his name, rewards those who keep his commandments and punishes those who do not.**
>
> Number 11 of the Thirteen Principles of Faith.

FACTFILE 47

HINDUISM AND CAPITAL PUNISHMENT

Most Hindus agree with capital punishment for murderers. They believe this because:

- the Vedas say that ahimsa does not apply to criminals;
- the Law of Manu says that a Hindu can kill someone to maintain social order;
- the Vahara Purana says that a king can execute criminals to restore the correct dharma;
- they would also use the non-religious arguments in favour of capital punishment.

Some Hindus do not agree with capital punishment because of Gandhi's teachings and the non-religious arguments against capital punishment.

> Take for example, a manacled man brought here by people shouting, 'He's a thief! He has committed a theft! Heat an axe for him!' Now, if he is guilty of the crime, then he turns himself into a lie uttering a falsehood and covering himself in falsehood, he takes hold of the axe and gets burnt upon which he is executed. If, on the other hand, he is innocent of the crime, then he turns himself into the truth; uttering the truth, he takes hold of the axe and is not burnt upon which he is released.

Chandogya Upanishad 6.16.1–2

> If any man thinks he slays, and if another thinks he is slain, neither knows the ways of truth. The Eternal in man cannot kill: the Eternal in man cannot die.

Bhagavad Gita 2:19

Questions

Factfile 32 Law and justice

1. Why is it important to have laws?
2. Give an example of something which is a sin but not a crime.
3. Give an example of something which is a crime but not a sin.

Factfile 33 Christianity and justice

Give three reasons why Christians should work for justice.

Factfiles 34, 35, 36 Islam, Judaism and Hinduism and justice

1. Choose one religion other than Christianity and give an outline of its teachings on justice.
2. 'All religious people should work for justice in the world.'
   a) Give two reasons for agreeing with this statement.
   b) Give two reasons for disagreeing with this statement.

Factfile 37 The nature of punishment

1. Write out definitions of three theories of punishment.
2. Have a class discussion on how to reduce crime.

Factfile 38 Christianity and punishment

1. Give three reasons why some Christians believe that reform should be the main punishment.
2. Give three reasons why some Christians believe in deterrence and retribution.

Factfiles 39, 40, 41 Islam, Judaism and Hinduism and punishment

1. Choose one religion other than Christianity and give an outline of its teachings on punishment.
2. 'Committing a sin is as bad as committing a crime.'
   a) Give two reasons for agreeing with this statement.
   b) Give two reasons for disagreeing with this statement.

Factfiles 43 Capital punishment and 44 Christianity and capital punishment

1. Give three arguments for capital punishment.
2. Give three arguments against capital punishment.
3. Give three reasons why many Christians are against capital punishment.

Factfiles 45, 46, 47 Islam, Judaism and Hinduism and capital punishment

1. Choose one religion other than Christianity and give an outline of its teachings on capital punishment.
2. 'No religious person can agree with capital punishment.'
   a) Give two reasons for agreeing with this statement.
   b) Give two reasons for disagreeing with this statement.

5 RELIGION AND MEDICAL ISSUES

FACTFILE 48

MEDICAL TREATMENTS FOR INFERTILITY

As many as 10% of couples in the UK have problems having children. Advances in embryo technology have led to these treatments being available:

IN-VITRO-FERTILISATION (IVF) – AN EGG IS TAKEN FROM THE MOTHER'S WOMB, FERTILISED IN A TEST TUBE AND PUT BACK IN THE WOMB.

ARTIFICIAL INSEMINATION BY HUSBAND (AIH) – WHEN THE HUSBAND'S SPERM IS PUT INTO THE WIFE'S WOMB BY MEDICAL MEANS.

ARTIFICIAL INSEMINATION BY DONOR (AID) – WHEN AN UNKNOWN MAN'S SPERM IS PUT INTO THE WIFE'S WOMB BY MEDICAL MEANS.

EGG DONATION – WHEN AN UNKNOWN WOMAN'S EGG AND THE HUSBAND'S SPERM ARE FERTILISED BY IVF AND PUT BACK IN THE WOMB.

EMBRYO DONATION – WHEN BOTH SPERM AND EGG ARE FROM UNKNOWN DONORS AND ARE FERTILISED BY IVF THEN PLACED IN THE WIFE'S WOMB.

SURROGACY – WHEN EITHER THE EGG AND SPERM OF HUSBAND AND WIFE, OR THE EGG OR SPERM OF HUSBAND OR WIFE AND AN UNKNOWN DONOR, ARE FERTILISED BY IVF AND THEN PLACED IN ANOTHER WOMAN'S WOMB AND THE BABY HANDED TO THE HUSBAND AND WIFE AFTER THE BIRTH.

These treatments are supervised by the Human Fertilisation and Embryology Authority, but many are not available on the NHS.

Sarah and Peter's triplets were conceived by IVF.

CHILDREN MAY GET RIGHT TO FIND DONOR PARENTS

Newspaper headline from 20 October 1998 when the Government ordered an investigation into sperm and egg donation which is now running at 2000 births a year.

Sarah and Peter have triplets who were conceived by IVF treatment after years of trying to have children.

When Sarah was asked how she and Peter felt when told they were unlikely to have children, she replied, 'As a woman I felt a failure. As a wife, I felt I was a dud.'

Peter, despite genuinely wanting children, was able to be more philosophical. He said, 'As a couple, we felt we were ready to move on to the next stage of our lives, but were suspended in childlessness. We felt real sadness.'

When asked how they felt when offered fertility treatment, Sarah said, 'We never felt it was wrong. We never thought it was tampering with the course of nature or against the will of God. We were delighted and optimistic when first offered treatment.

As far as life being parents is concerned, Sarah said, 'Life as parents is exhausting and hard work, but excellent. We feel a sense of the future and continuation. The babies give us a lot of happiness and laughter. They are a real gift to us.'

FACTFILE 49

CHRISTIANITY AND INFERTILITY

There are two Christian views on fertility treatments:

1 Roman Catholics and some other Christians ban all forms of embryo technology. They do this because:
- they all involve fertilisation taking place apart from the sex act and God intended procreation to come from sex;
- any process using IVF requires embryos to be created which are thrown away when not used and this is the same as abortion.

2 Other Christians accept IVF and AIH because:
- the egg and sperm are from the husband and wife;
- technology should be used to give couples the joy of children.

However, they are suspicious of all other techniques, though they have not banned them, because they involve problems of who the parents are and the children wanting information about the donors in later life.

All Christian Churches encourage childless couples to adopt.

> Techniques which allow someone other than the husband and wife to be involved in the making of a child are very wrong. Techniques which separate sex from the making of the baby, are unacceptable.

Catechism of the Catholic Church

> The Division of the Methodist Church which is responsible for advising the Church on medical ethics agrees that embryos up to fourteen days old can be used for infertility treatments and medical research.

Statement of the Methodist Church in What the Churches Say.

Adoption can give a couple children and then grandchildren.

Islam accepts IVF and AIH because:

- the egg and sperm are from the husband and wife;
- family is necessary for Muslims and technology can be used to help bring it about;
- the unused embryos are not foetuses until they are 14 days old and destroying them is not like abortion.

FACTFILE 50

ISLAM AND INFERTILITY

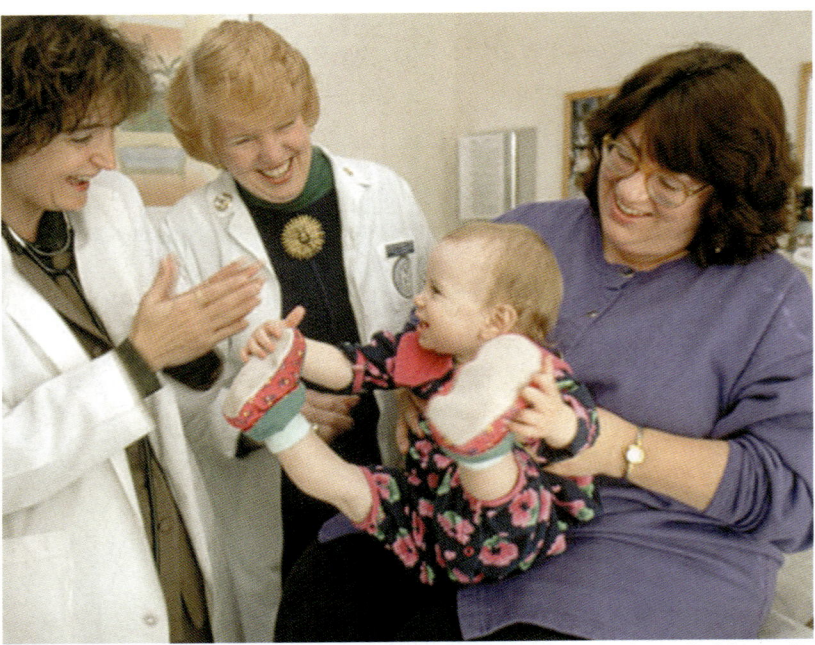

> As long as the husband's semen is used, it is permissible for doctors to use artificial means to fertilise the wife's egg.

Articles of Islamic Acts, Imam Al-Khoei.

Is it really wrong to conceive children by AID, as this child was?

Islam does not allow any forms of embryo technology because:

- they deny a child's right to know its natural parents;
- they are the same as adoption which is banned in Islam.

FACTFILE 49

JUDAISM AND INFERTILITY

> One day Elisha went to Shunem. And a well-to-do woman was there, who urged him to stay for a meal. So whenever he came by, he stopped there to eat ... 'What can be done for her?' Elisha asked. Gehazi said, 'Well, she has no son and her husband is old.'
> Then Elisha said, 'Call her.' So he called her, and she stood in the doorway ... 'About this time next year,' Elisha said, 'you will hold a son in your arms.'

2 Kings 4:8–15

IVF and AIH are accepted by all Jews and many would accept egg donation as long as the donor is Jewish. They believe this because:

- having children is very important in Judaism;
- the rabbis teach that humans can use the benefits of technology as long as they are within the mitzvot;
- the discarded embryos are not regarded as foetuses because they are not life until they are 14 days old.

Most Jews would not allow any other form of embryo technology because:

- AID is a form of adultery;
- children have a right to know who their natural parents are;
- whoever gives birth is the mother, so surrogacy is wrong.

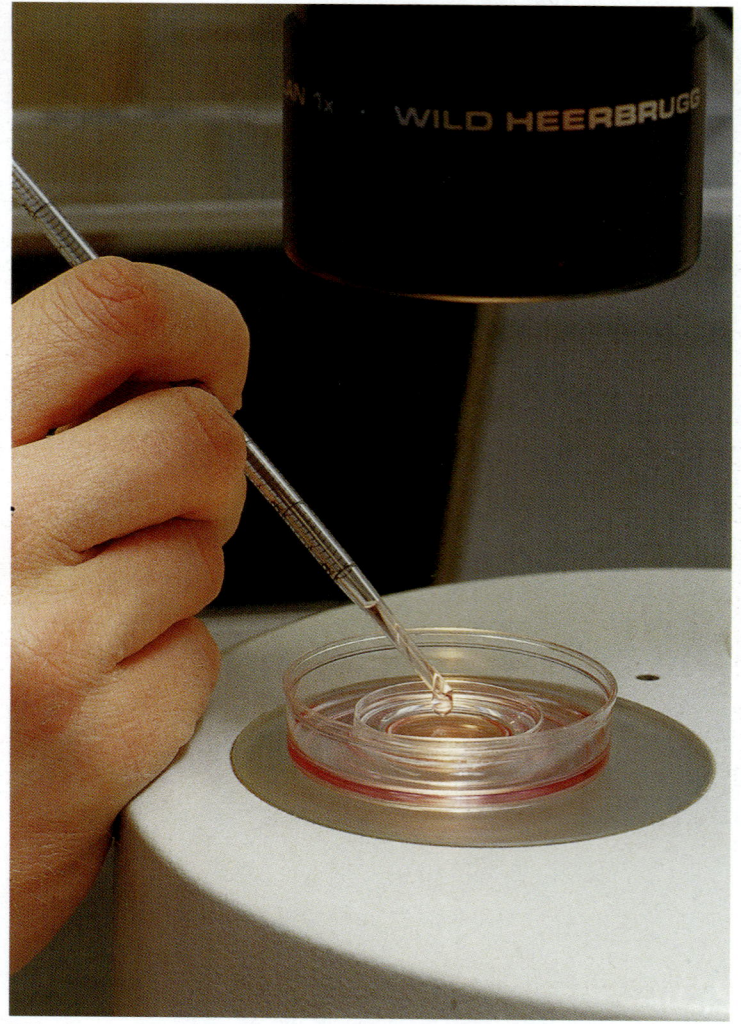

Life for some children now begins in a glass dish.

Hindus allow IVF and AID because:

- all Hindus are expected to have a family and technology can be used to bring this about;
- the egg and sperm are from the husband and wife;
- the discarded embryos had no soul transferred to them.

Aid and embryo donation are not allowed because:

- caste is passed down by the father.

Some Hindus would allow egg donation and surrogacy with strict controls.

FACTFILE 52

HINDUISM AND INFERTILITY

> The one who rules over both knowledge and ignorance ... alone presides over womb after womb, and thus over all visible forms and all the sources of birth.

Svetasvatara Upanishad 5:1–2

Should couples be allowed to adopt children over the Internet?

FACTFILE 53

GENETIC ENGINEERING

Genetic engineering means using scientific skills to change gene structure. In medical research it means changing gene structure to cure illnesses.

Genetic diseases affect large numbers of people and are responsible for such things as children not developing mentally, physical deformities and early deaths. Scientists are using research on gene development and the manipulation of genes to find cures for these diseases.

More recently discoveries in cloning have made it possible to use stem cells to grow healthy genes to replace ones which are not working properly. This involves using stem cells from embryos created for IVF, but not used.

DISABLED MPs PLEAD FOR CELL STEM RESEARCH

'Arrogant to deny sufferers of chronic diseases the chance of a cure,' says Labour MP. Addressing the House from her wheelchair, Anne Begg appealed to MPs with strong religious convictions not to deny those suffering from devastating illnesses the chance of a cure.

Newspaper report 16 December 2000.

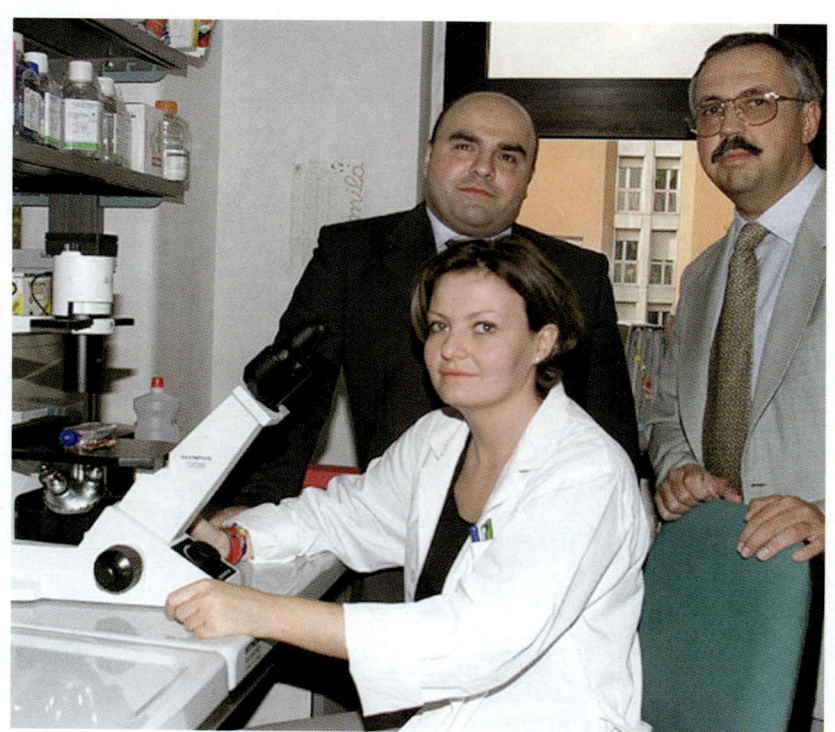

Stem cell researchers hope to produce cures for fatal diseases.

All genetic research into humans is controlled by the Human Fertilisation and Embryology Authority.

Non-religious arguments in favour of genetic engineering

- It could cure incurable diseases.
- It is an essential part of medical research.
- It is being done in most other countries so rich people would be able to use it anyway.

Non-religious arguments against genetic engineering

- We do not know what the long-term consequences are likely to be.
- If anything went wrong it could not be reversed.
- People might be made to have genetic tests for insurance, jobs etc, to check they did not have genes likely to cause illness.

FACTFILE 54

CHRISTIANITY AND GENETIC ENGINEERING

There are three main attitudes to genetic engineering among Christians:

1 Liberal Protestants support genetic engineering as long as it is done to cure disease and not to create perfect humans. They believe this because:

- Jesus showed that Christians should do all they can to cure disease;
- finding genetic cures is no different from finding drug cures;
- there is a difference between creating cells and creating people;
- embryos are not foetuses until they are 14 days old;
- they accept the non-religious arguments in favour of genetic engineering.

2 Roman Catholics, and some other Christians, agree with genetic research as long as it does not involve the use of embryos. They believe this because:

- Jesus showed that Christians should do all they can to cure disease;
- finding genetic cures is no different from finding drug cures;
- life begins at the moment of conception whether in a womb or a test tube and killing life is wrong;
- embryos have been produced by un-Christian means.

3 Some Christians are against all genetic research because:

- it is trying to play God which is a great sin;
- it is wrong to try to make the earth perfect, only heaven is perfect;
- they accept all the non-religious arguments against genetic engineering.

Should Christian leaders like the Archbishop of Westminster try to influence politicians in their decisions on genetic engineering?

We write to you as leaders of the Catholic community in Great Britain to protest against the Government's decision to allow stem cell cloning. This is very worrying to people of all faiths and none because it is wrong to create and destroy human lives just to make cells for research.

From a letter to *The Times* from the Roman Catholic Archbishops of Westminster and Glasgow, 14 December 2000

Jesus of Nazareth was a healer and where genetic manipulation is the means of healing diseases, it is to be welcomed.

Statement from the Methodist Church in *What the Churches Say*.

When you enter a town and are welcomed, eat what is set before you. Heal the sick who are there and tell them, 'The kingdom of God is near you.'

Luke 10:8–9

FACTFILE 55

ISLAM AND GENETIC ENGINEERING

> Abu Harairah reported that the Messenger of Allah said, 'Whenever any of you turns his eyes to one who has been given more of wealth and progress than he, let him look towards one who is inferior to himself.'

Hadith reported by Bukhari and Muslim.

Some Muslims are against all genetic engineering because:

- only God has the right to alter people's genetic make-up;
- it is playing God which is a great sin;
- embryo research involves abortion;
- they accept the non-religious arguments against genetic research.

Some Muslims agree with genetic engineering as long as it is done to cure diseases and not to create perfect people. They believe this because:

- the Qur'an and hadith teach that Muslims should do all they can to cure disease;
- it is no different from finding drug cures;
- there is a difference between creating cells and creating people;
- embryos are not foetuses until they are 14 days old so research on them is not abortion;
- they also accept the non-religious arguments in favour of genetic engineering.

The human genome project may give scientists all the information they need to create life.

FACTFILE 56

JUDAISM AND GENETIC ENGINEERING

Orthodox Jews agree with genetic engineering as long as it is done to cure disease and not create perfect people, but they do not allow research using embryos. They believe this because:

- the Talmud and Tenakh teach that Jews should do all they can to cure disease;
- it is no different from finding drug cures;
- there is a difference between creating cells and creating people;
- life begins at the moment of conception whether in a womb or a test tube;
- killing an embryo is the same as abortion;
- embryos for research have been created by methods with which Judaism disagrees.

Some Jews agree with all forms of genetic research because:

- the Talmud and Tenakh teach that Jews should do all they can to cure disease;
- it is no different from finding drug cures;
- there is a difference between creating cells and creating people;
- they believe that embryos are not life until they are 14 days old.

> **Whoever destroys a single life is considered as if he had destroyed the whole world, and whoever saves a single life as if he had saved the whole world.**

Mishnah

FACTFILE 57

HINDUISM AND GENETIC ENGINEERING

> When a man rightly sees, he sees no death, no sickness or distress. When a man rightly sees, he sees all.

Chandogya Upanishad 7.26.2

Most Hindus agree with genetic engineering as long as it is done to cure disease and not to create perfect humans. They believe this because:

- Hindus should do all they can to cure disease;
- discovering cures is part of the dharma of doctors;
- there is a difference between creating cells and creating people;
- embryos cannot be regarded as life until they are 14 days old.

Muscular dystrophy could be cured by stem cell research using information from the human genome project.

Some Hindus are opposed to all forms of genetic research because:

- it is breaking the law of karma. The genetic structure of people is what the law of karma says they should have on the basis of their previous lives.

FACTFILE 58

TRANSPLANT SURGERY

Transplant surgery is using organs from one person to replace defective organs in another. They may be taken from a living person (e.g. a kidney transplant) or a dead person (e.g. a heart transplant). Advances in medicine have made transplant surgery very effective.

Non-religious arguments in favour of transplant surgery

- It is an effective method of curing life-threatening or disabling diseases.
- It uses organs which would otherwise disappear.
- It allows people to help others after their death.

Non-religious arguments against transplant surgery

- It is very expensive and uses a lot of medical skill and money on a very few people.
- It raises moral problems about when a person is dead and whether surgeons try to keep alive someone whose organs can be used.
- It encourages the sale of organs from LDCs to the West.

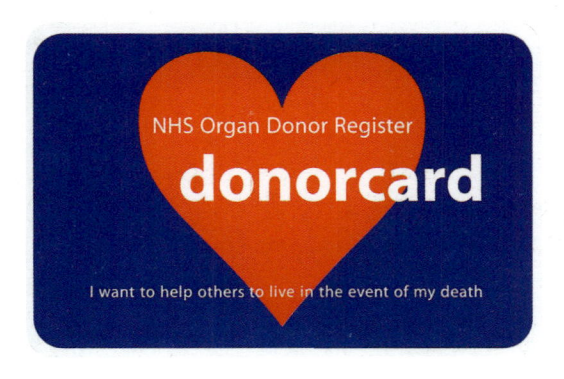

JODIE CLINGS TO LIFE AFTER SIAMESE TWINS SEPARATED

The Siamese twins, Jodie and Mary, were separated on 7 November 2000 using the skills of transplant surgery. The twins were joined at the base of their spines, but Mary's heart quickly failed and then her lungs so that she was using her sister as a life support machine. This was putting such a strain on Jodie's organs that doctors thought it likely they would both die within six months. However, the operation to separate the twins would kill Mary whilst saving Jodie's life. The doctors at St Mary's Hospital, Manchester, had to obtain a decision from the Court of Appeal before they could perform the operation against the wishes of the twins' Roman Catholic parents. Mary died during the operation, but Jodie survived and is likely to have a normal life.

NHS Organ Donor Register
donorcard
I want to help others to live in the event of my death

FACTFILE 59

CHRISTIANITY AND TRANSPLANT SURGERY

Most Christians agree with transplant surgery, but would disagree with organs being bought from poor people. They believe this because:

- those who believe in immortality of the soul believe the body is not needed after death;
- those who believe in resurrection believe that God will not need the organs to raise the body;
- leaving organs for others is a way of loving your neighbour;
- the Bible says the poor should not be exploited.

Some Christians agree with transplants using organs from living people, but not from dead people. They would also not allow payment for organs. They believe this because:

- transplanting organs from the dead to the living is playing God which is a great sin;
- donating your living organs is a way of loving your neighbour;
- paying for organs is exploiting the poor which is banned in the Bible.

Some Christians do not agree with transplants at all and do not carry donor cards because:

- they believe it ignores the sanctity of life;
- they believe it is playing God which is a great sin;
- they agree with all the non-religious arguments against transplants.

The funeral of Mary, the Siamese twin whose life was sacrificed to save her sister.

The case of the Siamese twins Mary and Jodie raised problems for Christians and transplant surgery.

Roman Catholics and many Evangelical Protestants argued that the twins should not be operated on because the surgeons would be murdering Mary.

Other Christians argued that the operation should be carried out because Mary was living off Jodie's organs and killing her and so the surgeons were only defending Jodie's life. The techniques of transplant surgery mean that doctors cannot leave such children to die.

FACTFILE 60

ISLAM AND TRANSPLANT SURGERY

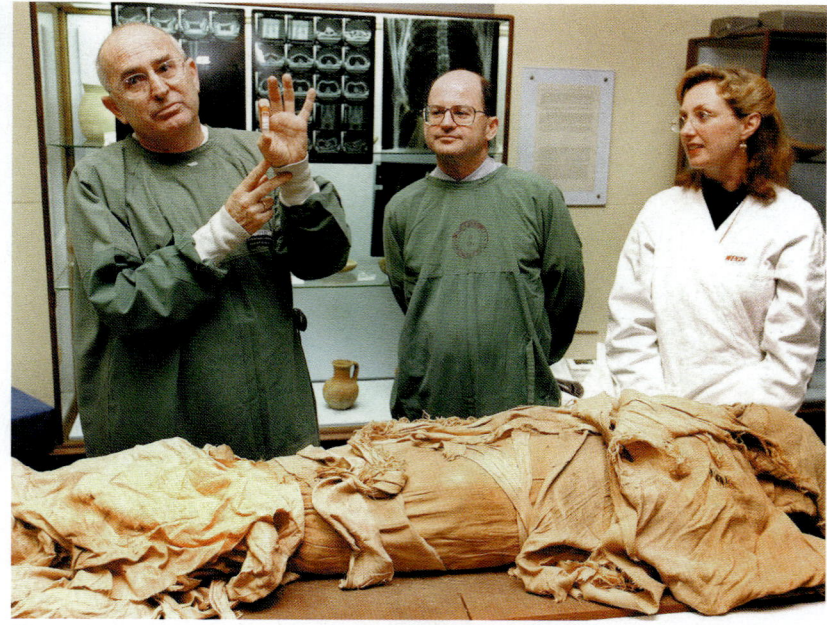

Post-mortems are required by British law when the cause of death is not certain, but they are disapproved of by Islam.

Most Muslims do not agree with transplant surgery because:

- the Shari'ah teaches that nothing should be removed from the body after death;
- it is playing God which is a great sin;
- the Qur'an teaches that only God has the right to give and take life;
- they would agree with all the non-religious arguments against transplants.

Some Muslims allow transplants from close relatives because:

- some Muslim lawyers have said it is allowed;
- the Muslim Law Council of the UK says that Muslims can carry donor cards and have transplants;
- Islam aims to do good and help people;
- they would agree with all the non-religious arguments in favour of transplants.

FACTFILE 61

JUDAISM AND TRANSPLANT SURGERY

Most Jews agree with transplants using living donors, but do not agree with using organs from dead people, or organs being paid for. They believe this because:

- organs such as the heart are an essential part of the individual God has created;
- organs from non-Jews would affect a person's Jewishness;
- organs from living donors are not as vital and can be used to obey the mitzvah to preserve life;
- paying for organs is exploiting the poor which is banned by the Tenakh.

Some Jews are against all forms of transplant surgery. They believe this because:

- transplanting organs is breaking the mitzvot on the sanctity of life;
- organs have been created by God for a specific person and cannot be swapped around;
- having non-Jewish organs could change a Jew into a non-Jew;
- they would also agree with all the non-religious arguments against transplants.

Heart transplants keep people alive through someone else's death.

FACTFILE 62

Hinduism and transplant surgery

Most Hindus agree with transplant surgery and would carry donor cards. They believe this because:

- the soul leaves the body on death, so what happens to the organs does not matter;
- the soul is the important part of any individual, so any organs added to the body do not matter;
- they agree with all the non-religious arguments in favour of transplants.

Some Hindus are against any form of transplant surgery because:

- transplants break the law of karma; if organs are diseased, that is part of that person's karma;
- taking an organ from someone else is doing violence to that person which is against the teaching of ahimsa;
- poor people will be tempted to sell their organs to provide money for the family.

Questions

Factfile 48 Medical treatments for infertility

1. Make a list of the treatments available for infertility.
2. Have a discussion in class on whether each treatment should be available.

Factfile 49 Christianity and infertility

1. Outline the Roman Catholic attitude to fertility treatments.
2. Outline the Protestant attitude to fertility treatments.

Factfiles 50, 51, 52 Islam, Judaism and Hinduism and infertility

1. Choose one religion other than Christianity and outline its teachings on infertility treatments.
2. 'If God wants people to have children, they will have them without using fertility treatments.'
   a) Give two reasons for agreeing with this statement.
   b) Give two reasons for disagreeing with this statement.

Factfile 53 Genetic engineering

1. Give three non-religious arguments against genetic engineering.
2. Give three non-religious arguments in favour of genetic engineeering.

Factfile 54 Christianity and genetic engineering

1. Give two reasons why some Christians are in favour of genetic engineering.
2. Give two reasons why some Christians are against genetic engineering.

Factfiles 55, 56, 57 Islam, Judaism and Hinduism and genetic engineering

1. Choose one religion other than Christianity and give an outline of its attitudes to genetic engineering.
2. 'Only God should interfere with our genes.'
   a) Give two reasons for agreeing with this statement.
   b) Give two reasons for disagreeing with this statement.

Factfile 58 Transplant surgery

Give an outline of the different types of transplant surgery.

Factfile 59 Christianity and transplant surgery

1. Give two reasons why some Christians are in favour of transplant surgery.
2. Give two reasons why some Christians are against transplant surgery.

Factfiles 60, 61, 62 Islam, Judaism and Hinduism and transplant surgery

1. Choose one religion other than Christianity and give an outline of its attitudes to transplant surgery.
2. 'No religious person can have a heart transplant.'
   a) Give two reasons for agreeing with this statement.
   b) Give two reasons for disagreeing with this statement.

6 RELIGION AND SCIENCE

FACTFILE 63

THE BIBLICAL COSMOLOGY

Cosmology is the study of how the universe came to be.

There are two accounts of creation in the Bible:

Genesis chapter 1 says God created the universe in six days in the order:

Day 1   heaven and earth,
Day 2   the seas,
Day 3   dry land and plants,
Day 4   sun, moon and stars,
Day 5   fish and birds,
Day 6   animals and humans.

Man and woman were made at the same time and humans were made in the 'image of God'.

Genesis chapter 2 says God created the universe in the order:

- heaven and earth,
- Adam,
- trees and vegetation,
- birds and animals,
- Eve from Adam's rib.

It then explains that because Adam and Eve disobeyed God, evil, suffering and death came into the world.

Adam and Eve in the Garden of Eden by Dora Holzhandler (1993).

Many Christians believe that the second account is just explaining the first and that both are the word of God.

Other Christians believe that the two accounts are both stories to explain how God created the world and they are not meant to be taken literally.

FACTFILE 64

THE ISLAMIC COSMOLOGY

There are two Muslim views on the origins of the universe and humans:

1 The traditional view

Some Muslims believe that because there are references in the Qur'an to God creating the universe in six days, and to Adam and his wife as the first humans:

- God created the universe and everything in it in six days;
- God created Adam and his wife as the first humans;
- all humans are descended from Adam and Eve.

2 The modern view

Some Muslims (e.g. Dr Maurice Bucaille in 'The Qur'an and Modern Science') claim that God created the universe in a more gradual way which fits in with evolution. They believe this because:

- the Arabic words in the Qur'an mean six ages not six days;
- there is no order of creation in the Qur'an;
- the Qur'an clearly shows that in these six ages, God created the universe, then life on earth and finally humans.

Front cover of Qur'an and Modern Science.

The Jewish Cosmology is the same as the Biblical Cosmology in Factfile 63 because Genesis is part of the Jewish Torah.

FACTFILE 65

THE JEWISH COSMOLOGY

FACTFILE 66

THE HINDU COSMOLOGY

There are many different accounts of how the universe and humans began in Hinduism, but the two main ones are:

1 The cosmology based on myths

One account is based on stories in the Vedas. It says that the whole universe came from Purusha who sacrificed himself to create the universe. The story is also the basis of the caste system because the higher castes came from the higher parts of his body.

Many Hindus believe the universe is in continual creation.

2 The cosmology based on ideas

The other account is based on philosophical ideas in the Upanishads. It claims that Brahman is the force behind the universe and the creation of the universe is like samsara. The universe comes into being, it lives, it dies, then it is reborn and so on in an unending process.

Scientific discoveries have led to a cosmology based on science rather than religion.

Science says that matter is eternal and has always existed. It claims that:

- about 15 billion years ago the matter of the universe exploded (the Big Bang).
- after the explosion, scientific forces such as gravity compressed the exploded matter into stars and solar systems.
- as part of this process our solar system was formed about 5 billion years ago.
- chemical reactions on the earth led to life forms beginning and the process of evolution over 2.5 billion years led to the arrival of humans about 2.5 million years ago.

FACTFILE 67

THE SCIENTIFIC COSMOLOGY

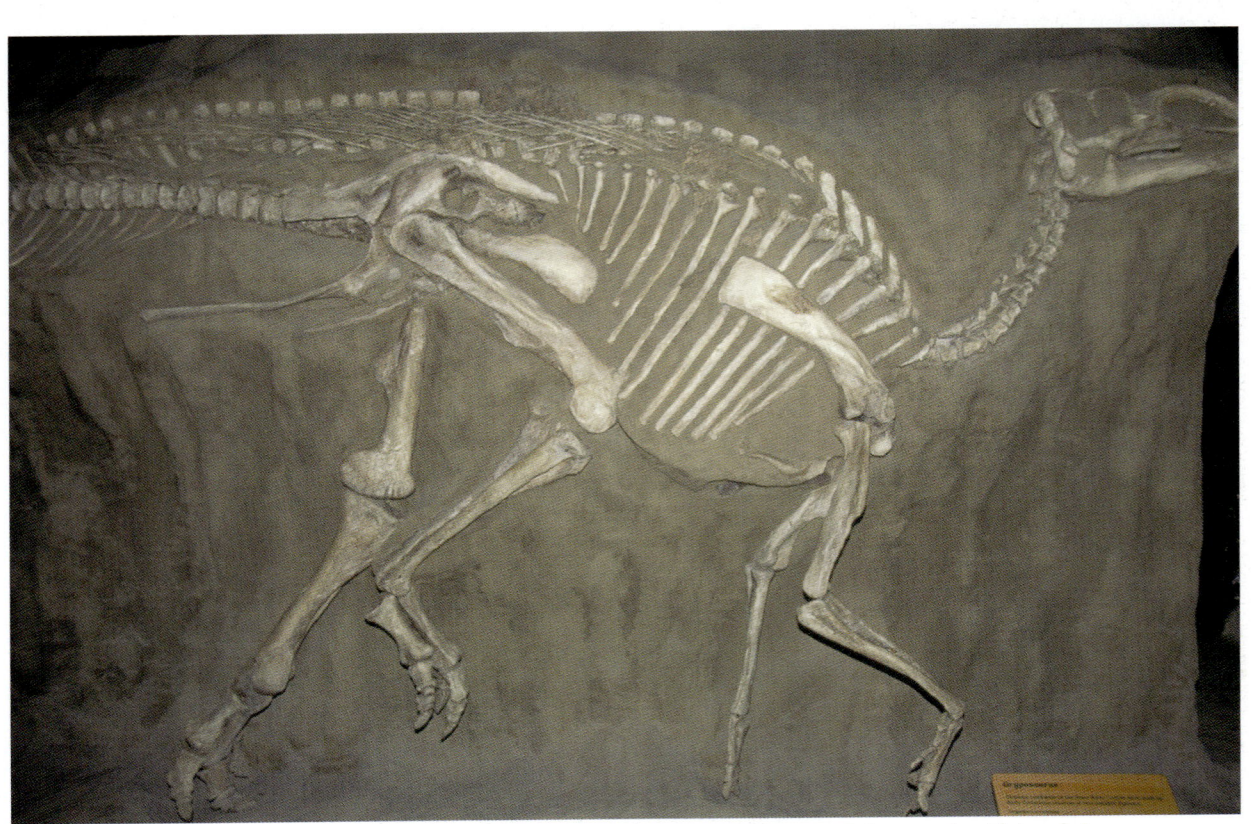

Many scientists claim dinosaurs are evidence for the scientific cosmology.

FACTFILE 68

RELIGIOUS ATTITUDES TO THE SCIENTIFIC COSMOLOGY

The scientific cosmology does not need God to explain the universe or the existence of humans and religion has responded in a variety of ways.

Christian responses

Many Christians simply ignore the scientific cosmology, but those who think about it have responded in the following ways:

1 Creationism

Some Christians reject the scientific cosmology. They say it is wrong and Genesis is correct. They claim that the evidence for Big Bang, evolution, etc, is better explained by creationism – the idea that at the moment when God created the earth, the Grand Canyon would have looked 2 billion years old even though it was only a second old.

2 Conservatism

Some Christians claim that both the Bible and science are correct and that one of God's days could be millions or billions of years.

A spiral galaxy forming in the aftermath of the Big Bang.

3 Liberalism

Some Christians believe that the scientific cosmology is the true one and the Bible is just a story. They believe that the scientific cosmology needs God to make it work because:

- if the Big Bang had been a micro-second earlier or later the universe would not have developed;
- the way exploding stars are needed to spread chemicals needs someone to organise it;
- the way life requires carbon to bond with other atoms could not happen by chance.

They believe that God set off the Big Bang at just the right micro-second for the universe and humans to develop.

> **Your guardian Lord is God who created the heavens and the earth in six days and is firmly established on the throne of authority.**
>
> *Surah 7:54*

> **God saw all that he had made, and it was very good. And there was evening and there was morning – the sixth day.**
>
> *Genesis 1:31*

> **Matter evolves into material form by virtue of its own potentialities and requires no other agency to effect the transformation.**
>
> *Vishnu Purana 1.4.52*

> The Qur'an shows the evolution of the heavens and the earth. It speaks of an original gaseous mass which split to form the universe.
>
> *The Qur'an and Modern Science*, M. Bucaille.

> The Big Bang theory implies the act of a God.
>
> *A Brief History of Time*, Stephen Hawking

Muslim responses

Muslims who believe in six day creation believe that the Qur'an is correct and that science is wrong.

Muslims who believe in six age creation believe that the scientific cosmology and the Qur'an are the same. God created the matter of the universe and the laws of science which led to the creation of the universe and life. They believe that God intervened to breathe his life into humans.

Hindu responses

Some Hindus never think about the scientific cosmology. They believe the Purusha story is the way creation happened.

Many Hindus believe that the scientific cosmology is just the same as those in the Upanishads. The Big Bang is the way Brahman began the current universe. The universe will eventually contract and then explode again to form a new universe and so on for ever.

Jewish responses

A few Orthodox Jews reject the scientific cosmology. They say it is wrong and Genesis is correct. They claim that the evidence for the Big Bang, evolution etc is better explained by creationism – the idea that at the moment when God created the earth, the Grand Canyon would have looked two billion years old even though it was only a second old.

Most Orthodox Jews and some Liberal Jews claim that both the Bible and science are correct and that one of God's days could be millions or billions of years.

Most Liberal Jews believe that the scientific cosmology is the true one and the Bible is just a story. They believe that the scientific cosmology needs God to make it work. They believe that God set off the Big Bang at just the right micro-second for the universe and humans to develop.

> What is revealed of the divine in the human life of Jesus is also to be discerned in the cosmic story of creation.
>
> *Science and Creation*, J. Polkinghorne

> The point is that, for the existence of any forms of life that we may conceive, the necessary environment, whatever its nature, must be complex and dependent on a multiplicity of coincident conditions, such as are not reasonably attributable to blind forces or to pure mechanism.
>
> F R Tennant quoted in *The Existence of God*, ed. J. Hick.

FACTFILE 69

HOW SCIENCE AND RELIGION ARE CONNECTED

There are many differences between science and religion:

- science deals with the material: religion deals with the spiritual;
- science is based on facts: religion is based on beliefs;
- science is based on recent discoveries: religion is based on holy books written thousands of years ago.

However, there are also many similarities:

Science	Religion
• is based on everything having an explanation;	• believes everything can be explained by God;
• believes invisible forces affect the way things behave e.g. gravity, magnetism;	• believes that God is an invisible force which affects everything;
• science is based on belief – nothing happens by chance, everything can be explained by scientific methods.	• religion is based on belief – nothing happens by chance, everything can be explained by God.

> **The heavens declare the glory of God; the skies proclaim the work of his hands.**
>
> *Psalm 19:1*

The beauty and order of the solar system lead many astronomers to believe in God.

123

> **Behold! In the creation of the heavens and the earth; in the alternation of the night and the day ... In the rain which God sends down from the skies and the life which he gives therewith to an earth which is dead; in the beasts of all kinds ... here indeed are signs for a people that is wise.'**
>
> Surah 2:164

Many scientists have been led to believe in God through their science. They believe that

- the beauty and order of science and;
- the way that mathematical principles seem to lie at the heart of science

mean there must be something which has organised the universe in this way.

> Nature is as divine a text as the Holy Scriptures.

Galileo

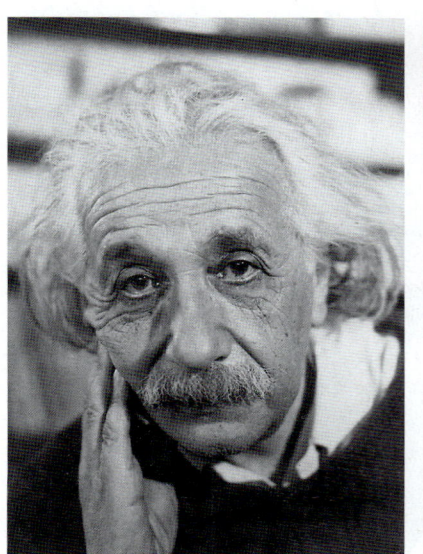

> God does not play dice.

Einstein

Einstein also said that science cannot work properly without a religious belief and religion which ignores science is blind to reality.

Einstein.

QUESTIONS

Factfile 63 The biblical cosmology

1. What is meant by cosmology?
2. Give an outline of the cosmology in Genesis chapter 1.
3. Give an outline of the cosmology in Genesis chapter 2.

Factfiles 64, 65, 66 The Islamic, Jewish and Hindu cosmology

Choose one religion other than Christianity and give an outline of its traditional cosmology.

Factfile 67 The scientific cosmology

1. Give an outline of the scientific cosmology.
2. Why do some people think the scientific cosmology disproves religion?

Factfile 68 Religious attitudes to the scientific cosmology

1. Outline two Christian responses to the scientific cosmology.
2. Outline the response of one religion other than Christianity to the scientific cosmology.
3. 'God made the world.'
   a) Give two reasons for agreeing with this statement.
   b) Give two reasons for disagreeing with this statement.

Factfile 69 How religion and science are connected

1. Give an outline of the differences between science and religion.
2. Give an outline of the similarities between science and religion.
3. 'Science has disproved religion.'
   a) Give two reasons for agreeing with this statement.
   b) Give two reasons for disagreeing with this statement.

Useful addresses

Amnesty International
99–119 Roseberry Avenue
London EC1R 4RE

Animals in Medicine Research Information Centre
12 Whitehall
London SW1A 2DY

BBC Religious Broadcasting
New Broadcasting House
Oxford Road
Manchester M60 1SJ

Board of Deputies of British Jews
Woburn House
Upper Woburn Place
London WC1H 0EP

The Bourne Trust
(Christian group helping prisoners and their families)
Lincoln House
1 Brixton Road
London SW9 6DE

CAFOD
2 Romero Close
Stockwell Road
London SW9 9TY

Catholic Truth Society
38–40 Eccleston Square
London SW1V 1PD

Channel 4 TV
60 Charlotte Street
London W1P 2AX

The Children's Society
Edward Rudolf House
Margery Street
London W1X 0JL

Christian Aid
PO Box 100
London SW1 7RT

Christian Animal Rights Education
PO Box 407
Sheffield S1 1ED

Christian Communication Bureau
4 Hindes Road
Harrow
Middlesex HA1 1SJ

Christian Ecology Group
c/o Mrs Joan Hart
17 Burns Gardens
Lincoln LN2 4LJ

Christian Education Movement
Royal Buildings
Victoria Street
Derby DE1 1GW

Church of England Information Office
Church House
Dean's Yard
London SW1P 3NZ

ISKCON (International Society for Krishna Consciousness)
10 Soho Street
London W1V 5FA

Islamic Foundation
Markfield Dawah Centre
Ratby Lane
Markfield
Leicester LE67 9RN

Islamic Relief
19 Rea Street South
Birmingham B5 6LB

Islamic Vision
481 Coventry Road
Birmingham B10 0JS

Jewish Care
221 Golders Green Road
London NW11

Jewish Education Bureau
8 Westcombe Avenue
Leeds LS8 2BS

Muslim Aid
PO Box 3
London N7 8LR

Muslim Educational Trust
130 Stroud Green Road
London N4 3RZ

Muslim Law (Shari'ah)
20–22 Creffield Road
London W5

Office of the Chief Rabbi
Adler House
Tavistock Square
London WC1H 9HN

Ramakrishna Vedanta Centre
Unity House
Blind Lane
Bourne End
Berkshire SL8 5LG

RSPCA
Causeway
Horsham
West Sussex RH12 1HG

Salvation Army Headquarters
101 Queen Victoria Street
London EC4P

The Swaminarayan Hindu Mission
Shri Swaminarayan Mandir
105–119 Brentfield Road
Neasden
London NW10 8SP

Tearfund
11 Station Road
Teddington
Middlesex TW11 9AA

Union of Liberal and Progressive Jews
Montague Centre
109 Westfield Street
London W1P 5RP

World Jewish Relief
Drayton House
30 Gordon Street
London WC1H 0AN

INDEX

Acid rain 30
Animal rights 44–45
    Christianity 46
    Hinduism 49
    Islam 47
    Judaism 48

Beveridge Report 24
Bhagavad Gita 13, 49, 58, 59, 78, 92
Bible — nature of 7, 8
Bible references 19, 22, 23, 26, 27, 35, 38, 39, 46, 48, 54, 55, 57, 62, 65, 67, 76, 80, 81, 83, 88, 89, 91, 98, 103, 122, 123
Bullying 62–63

Capital punishment 87
    Christianity 88–89
    Hinduism 92
    Islam 90
    Judaism 91
Catechism of the Catholic Church 7, 16, 18, 19, 23, 27, 36, 55, 65, 96
Conflict
    areas of 52–53
    causes of 64
Cosmology Biblical 114–115
    Hindu 118
    Islamic 116
    Jewish 117
    Religious attitudes 120–122
    Scientific 119
Crime and punishment 70–71

Deforestation 31
Dharma 78, 84

Electoral system 20–21
Environment 29–34
    and religious groups 42
    Christianity 35–36
    Hinduism 40–41
    Islam 37
    Judaism 38–39
Eutrophication 30

Forgiveness
    Christianity 65
    Hinduism 68
    Islam 66
    Judaism 67

General Synod 18, 36

Genetic engineering 100–101
    Christianity 102–103
    Hinduism 106
    Islam 104
    Judaism 105
God (nature of)
    Christianity 7
    Hinduism 13
    Islam 9
    Judaism 11
Golden Rule 26
Greenhouse effect 29

Holy War (jihad) 56

Infertility 94–95
    Christianity 96
    Hinduism 99
    Islam 97
    Judaism 98
Jewish National Fund 43
Jubilee 2000 23, 72
July Bomb Plot 86
Just War
    Christian 55
    Hindu 58
Justice
    Christianity 71–73
    Hinduism 78
    Islam 74–75
    Judaism 76–77

Law 70–71, 81
Law of Manu 49, 92, 99

Moksha 13, 68, 78
Moral issues 7, 9, 11, 13, 15
Multi–faith society 22
Muslim Aid 42, 74

Natural resources, problems 32

Orthodox Jews 12, 105

Pacifism 54, 58
Pax Christi 60–61
Peace and conflict 51–53
    Christianity 54–55
    Hinduism 58–59
    Islam 56
    Judaism 57
Politics and Religion 22–23

Pollution, dangers 29–31
Prisoners of conscience 85–86
Protestants 7, 8, 102
Punishment
    Christianity 80–81
    deterrence 79, 81, 82, 83, 84
    Hinduism 84
    Islam 82
    Judaism 83
    protection 79, 81, 82, 83, 84, 87
    reform 79, 80, 82, 84, 88
    retribution 79, 82, 83, 84, 87, 88

Qur'an
    nature of 9
    references 37, 47, 56, 63, 66, 74, 75, 82, 104, 122, 124

Radioactive pollution 31
Reform Jews 12
Roman Catholics 7, 8, 60, 96, 102

Science and Religion 114–115
Shari'ah 9, 10, 37, 74, 75, 90, 104, 110
Social responsibility 16–27
Stem cell research 100

Talmud 11, 57, 76, 77, 91, 105
Target Earth 42
Tawhid 37
Tenakh
    nature of 11
    references 57, 76, 105
Torah 76, 83, 91
Transplant surgery 107
    Christianity 108–109
    Islam 110
    Judaism 111
    Hinduism 112

Upanishads 13, 40, 68, 99, 106

Vedas 13

Welfare State 24–27
World Jewish Relief 76, 77